Northwest England

Nicola Gibbs

Credits

Footprint credits
Editorial: Nicola Gibbs
Maps: Kevin Feeney
Proofreader: Sophie Jones
Cover: Pepi Bluck

Publisher: Patrick Dawson
Managing Editor: Felicity Laughton
Advertising: Elizabeth Taylor
Sales and marketing: Kirsty Holmes

Photography credits
Front cover: Shahid Khan/Dreamstime.com
Back cover: Alastair Wallace/
Shutterstock.com

Printed in Great Britain by CPI Antony Rowe,
Chippenham, Wiltshire

Publishing information
Footprint *Focus Northwest England*
1st edition
© Footprint Handbooks Ltd
April 2013

ISBN: 978 1 909268 19 7
CIP DATA: A catalogue record for this book
is available from the British Library

® Footprint Handbooks and the Footprint
mark are a registered trademark of Footprint
Handbooks Ltd

Published by Footprint
6 Riverside Court
Lower Bristol Road
Bath BA2 3DZ, UK
T +44 (0)1225 469141
F +44 (0)1225 469461
footprinttravelguides.com

Distributed in the USA by Globe Pequot Press,
Guilford, Connecticut

MIX
Paper from
responsible sources
FSC® C013604
www.fsc.org

Contains ...
© Crown ...
right 2013 ...

... Northwest
... m Footprint's
... researched
... y-Faussett.

**London Borough
of Southwark**

SK 2341409	X	
Askews & Holts	14 MAY - 2013	
914. 2704 TRAV	£7.99	

Contents

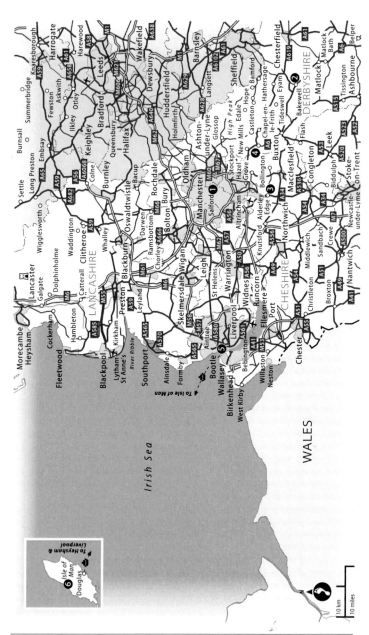

The northwest of England is an unusual hotchpotch of broad plains, industrial cities, pre-Roman history and trendy post-industrial chic. Shaped by the Industrial Revolution of the 18th and 19th centuries, Manchester, Liverpool and Lancashire were central to the development of industry in England. The bubble burst, though, and in the late 19th century the Northwest became synonymous with dark, desolate mills and urban decay.

These days things have moved on. Manchester and Liverpool are lively cities much aided by the 2002 Commonwealth Games which allowed the almost total redevelopment of Manchester city centre and the creation of new museums like the Imperial War Museum of the North. They are two of the country's hot spots for nightlife, but that's not to say that there's nothing to do round here during the day. The Peak District National Park is the jewel of the region, curving around the spine of the Pennines with scenic views and wonderful walking country within an hour's journey of the city. The Cheshire Plain to the southwest is lush countryside with a depth of history; the Roman town of Chester is an ideal stop-over on the way to the Lake District.

One thing's for sure, this region has finally shrugged off the ghosts of the past, rejoicing in its heritage with an eye on the future. Whether looking over the hills of the Peak District or drinking beer in a canalside bar, take a moment to consider whether it really is all that grim up north.

Planning your trip

Best time to visit England

The weather in England is notoriously unpredictable. It is generally better between May and September, although it can be gloriously hot in April and cold and damp in August. The west of the country is milder and wetter than the east, whilst northern and mountainous areas are usually the coldest.

Transport in England

Compared to the rest of Western Europe, public transport in England is expensive and can be unreliable. Rail tickets, in particular, should be booked well in advance to avoid paying extortionate prices. Coach travel is cheaper but slower, and can be hampered by traffic problems particularly around London, Manchester and Birmingham. If you plan to spend much time in rural areas, it may be worth hiring a car, especially if you are travelling as a couple or group. A useful website for all national public transport information is Traveline ① *T0871-200 2233, www.traveline.info.*

Air
England is a small country and air travel isn't necessary to get around. However, with traffic a problem around the cities, some of the cheap fares offered by budget airlines may be very attractive. There are good connections between **London** and all the regional airports, although travel from region to region without coming through London is more difficult and expensive. Bear in mind the time and money it will take you to get to the airport (including check-in times) when deciding whether flying is really going to be a better deal.

Airport information National Express operates a frequent service between London's main airports. **London Heathrow Airport** ① *16 miles west of London between junctions 3 and 4 on the M4, T0844-335 1801, www.heathrowairport.com,* is the world's busiest international airport and it has five terminals, so when leaving London, it's important to check which terminal to go to before setting out for the airport. To get into central London, the cheapest option is the London Underground Piccadilly Line (50 minutes). The fastest option is **Heathrow Express** ① *T0845-6001515, www.heathrowexpress.com,* taking 15-20 minutes. There is a train service **Heathrow Connect** ① *Heathrow T0845-748 4950, www.heathrowconnect.com,* which takes 25 minutes. Coaches to destinations all over the country are run by **National Express** ① *T0871-781 8181, www.nationalexpress.com.* There are also buses to Oxford (www.oxfordbus.co.uk), to Reading for trains to Bristol and southwest England (www.railair.com), to Watford for trains to the north of England (www.greenline.co.uk) and to West London (www.tfl.gov.uk). A taxi to central London takes one hour and costs £45-70.

    London Gatwick Airport ① *28 miles south of London, off junction 9 on the M23, T0844-892 03222, www.gatwickairport.com,* has two terminals, North and South, with all the usual facilities. To central London, there is the **Gatwick Express** ① *T0845-850 1530,*

Don't miss...

www.gatwickexpress.com, *from £17.75 single online*, which takes 30 minutes. **Thameslink** rail services run from King's Cross, Farringdon, Blackfriars and London Bridge stations. Contact **National Rail Enquiries** (T0845-748 4950, www.nationalrail.co.uk) for further information. **EasyBus** (www.easybus.co.uk) is the cheapest option, with prices starting at £9.99 for a single, taking just over an hour. A taxi takes a similar time and costs from around £60.

   London City Airport ① *Royal Dock, 6 miles (15 mins' drive) east of the City of London, T020-7646 0000, www.londoncityairport.com*. Take the **Docklands Light Railway** (DLR) to Canning Town (seven minutes) for the **Jubilee line** or a connecting shuttle bus service. A taxi into central London will cost around £35.

   London Luton Airport ① *30 miles north of central London, 2 miles off the M1 at junction 10, southeast of Luton, Beds, T01582-405100, www.london-luton.co.uk*. Regular **First Capital Connect** trains run to central London; a free shuttle bus service operates between the airport terminal and the station. **Green Line** (www.greenline.co.uk) coaches run to central London, as does **easyBus** (www.easybus.co.uk). **National Express** (www.national express.com) operates coaches to many destinations. A taxi takes 50 minutes, costing from £70.

   Stansted Airport ① *35 miles northeast of London (near Cambridge) by junction 8 of the M11, T0844-335 1803, www.stanstedairport.com*. **Stansted Express** (T0845-600 7245, www.stanstedexpress.com) runs trains to London's Liverpool Street Station (45 minutes, £22.50 single). **EasyBus** (www.easybus.co.uk, from £2), **Terravision** (www.terravision.eu, £9) and **National Express** (www.nationalexpress.com, from £8.50) run to central London (55 minutes to East London, 1 hour 30 minutes to Victoria). A taxi to central London takes around an hour to 1 hour 30 minutes, depending on traffic, and costs around £99.

   Manchester International Airport ① *junction 5 of the M56, T0871-271 0711, www.manchesterairport.co.uk*. The airport is well served by public transport, with trains to and from Manchester Piccadilly as well as direct and connecting services from all over the north of England. **National Express** (www.nationalexpress.com) runs routes covering the whole of the UK. A taxi into the city centre should cost around £20.

   Birmingham International Airport (BHX) ① *8 miles east of the city centre at junction 6 on the M42, T0871-222 0072, www.birminghamairport.co.uk*. A taxi into the centre should cost from £25. Several trains per hour run the free 10-minute Air-Rail Link to Birmingham International Station, and other connections across England and Wales can be made by rail or coach, with **National Express** (www.nationalexpress.com).

Rail

National Rail Enquiries ① *T08457-484950, www.nationalrail.co.uk*, are quick and courteous with information on rail services and fares but not always accurate, so double check. They can't book tickets but will provide you with the relevant telephone number. The website, www.thetrainline.co.uk, also shows prices clearly.

Railcards There are a variety of railcards which give discounts on fares for certain groups. Cards are valid for one year and most are available from main stations. You need two passport photos and proof of age or status. A **Young Person's Railcard** is for those aged 16-25 or full-time students aged 26+ in the UK. Costs £28 for one year and gives 33% discount on most train tickets and some other services (www.16-25railcard.co.uk). A **Senior Citizen's Railcard** is for those aged over 60, is the same price and offers the same discounts as a Young Person's Railcard (www.senior-railcard.co.uk). A **Disabled Person's Railcard** costs £20 and gives 33% discount to a disabled person and one other. Pick up an application form from stations and send it to Disabled Person's Railcard Office, PO Box 11631, Laurencekirk AB30 9AA. It may take up to 10 working days to be delivered, so apply in advance (www.disabledpersons-railcard.co.uk). A **Family & Friends Railcard** costs £28 and gives 33% discount on most tickets for up to four adults travelling together, and 60% discount for up to four children. It's available to buy online as well as in most stations.

Road

Bus and coach Travelling by bus takes longer than the train but is much cheaper. Road links between cities and major towns in England are excellent, but far less frequent in more remote rural areas, and a number of companies offer express coach services day and night. The main operator is **National Express** ① *T08717-818178, www.national express.com*, which has a nationwide network with over 1000 destinations. Tickets can be bought at bus stations, from a huge number of agents throughout the country or online. Sample return fares if booked in advance: London to Manchester (4½ hours) £28, London to Cambridge (2½ hours) £12. **Megabus** ① *T0900-160 0 900 (61p a min from BT landlines, calls from other networks may be higher), http://megabus.com*, is a cheaper alternative with a more limited service.

Full-time students, those aged under 25 or over 60 or those registered disabled, can buy a coach card for £10 which is valid for one year and gets you a 30% discount on all fares. Children normally travel for half price, but with a **Family Card** costing £16, two children travel free with two adults. Available to overseas passport holders, the **Brit Xplorer Pass** offers unlimited travel on all National Express buses. Passes cost from £79 for seven days, £139 for 14 days and £219 for its month-long **Rolling Stone Pass**. They can be bought from major airports and bus terminals.

Car Travelling with your own private transport is the ideal way to explore the country, particularly in areas with limited public transport. This allows you to cover a lot of ground in a short space of time and to reach remote places. The main disadvantages are rising fuel costs, parking and traffic congestion. The latter is particularly heavy on the M25 which encircles London, the M6 around Birmingham and the M62 around Manchester. The M4 and M5 motorways to the West Country can also become choked at weekends and bank holidays and the roads in Cornwall often resemble a glorified car park during the summer.

Motoring organizations can help with route planning, traffic advice, insurance and breakdown cover. The two main ones are: the **Automobile Association (AA)** ① *T0800-085 2721, emergency number T0800-887766, www.theaa.com,* which offers a year's breakdown cover starting at £38, and the **Royal Automobile Club (RAC)** ① *T0844-273 4341, emergency number T08000-828282, www.rac.co.uk,* which has a year's breakdown cover starting at £31.99. Both have cover for emergency assistance. You can still call the emergency numbers if you're not a member, but you'll have to a pay a large fee.

Vehicle hire

Car hire is expensive and the minimum you can expect to pay is around £100 per week for a small car. Always check and compare conditions, such as mileage limitations, excess payable in the case of an accident, etc. Small, local hire companies often offer better deals than the larger multinationals. Most companies prefer payment with a credit card – some insist on it – otherwise you'll have to leave a large deposit (£100 or more). You need to have had a full driver's licence for at least a year and to be aged between 21 (25 for some companies) and 70.

Bicycle

Cycling is a pleasant if slightly hazardous way to see the country. Although conditions for cyclists are improving, with a growing network of cycle lanes in cities, most other roads do not have designated cycle paths, and cyclists are not allowed on motorways. You can load your bike onto trains, though some restrictions apply during rush hour. See the website www.ctc.org.uk for information on routes, restrictions and facilities.

Where to stay in England

Accommodation can mean anything from being pampered to within an inch of your life in a country house spa hotel to glamping in a yurt. If you have the money, then the sky is very much the limit in terms of sheer splendour and excess. We have tried to give as broad a selection as possible to cater for all tastes and budgets, with a bias towards those that offer that little bit extra in terms of character.

If you can't find what you're after, or if someone else has beaten you to the draw, then the tourist information centres (TICs) will help find accommodation for you. Some offices charge a small fee (usually £1) for booking a room, while others ask you to pay a deposit of 10% which is deducted from your first night's bill. Details of town and city TICs are given throughout the guide.

Accommodation will be your greatest expense, particularly if you are travelling on your own. Single rooms are in short supply and many places are reluctant to let a double room to one person, even when they're not busy. Single rooms typically cost around 75% of the price of a double room, although some establishments do not charge single supplements.

Hotels, guesthouses and B&Bs

Area tourist boards publish accommodation lists that include campsites, hostels, self-catering accommodation, hotels, guesthouses and bed and breakfasts (B&Bs). Places participating in the VisitEngland system will have a plaque displayed outside which shows their grading, determined by a number of stars ranging from one to five. These

Price codes

Where to stay

££££	over £160	**£££**	£90-160
££	£50-90	**£**	under £50

Prices include taxes and service charge, but not meals. They are based on a one-night stay in a double room in high season.

Restaurants

£££	over £30	**££**	£15-30	**£**	under £15

Prices refer to the cost of a two-course meal for one person, without a drink.

reflect the level of facilities, as well as the quality of hospitality and service. However, do not assume that a B&B, guesthouse or hotel is no good because it is not listed by the tourist board. They simply don't want to pay to be included in the system, and some of them may offer better value.

Hotels At the top end of the scale there are some fabulously luxurious hotels, some in beautiful locations. Some are converted mansions or castles, and offer a chance to enjoy a taste of aristocratic grandeur and style. At the lower end of the scale, there is often little to choose between cheaper hotels and guesthouses or B&Bs. The latter often offer higher standards of comfort and a more personal service, but many smaller hotels are really just guesthouses, and are often family run and every bit as friendly. Rooms in most mid-range to expensive hotels almost always have bathrooms en suite. Many upmarket hotels offer excellent room-only deals in the low season. An efficient last-minute hotel booking service is www.laterooms.com, which specializes in weekend breaks. Also note that many hotels offer cheaper rates for online booking through agencies such as www.lastminute.com.

Guesthouses Guesthouses are often large, converted family homes with up to five or six rooms. They tend to be slightly more expensive than B&Bs, charging between £30 and £50 per person per night, and though they are often less personal, usually provide better facilities, such as en suite bathroom, TV in each room, free Wi-Fi and private parking. Many guesthouses offer evening meals, though this may have to be requested in advance.

Bed and breakfasts (B&Bs) B&Bs usually provide the cheapest private accommodation. At the bottom end of the scale you can get a bedroom in a private house, a shared bathroom and a huge cooked breakfast from around £25 per person per night. Small B&Bs may only have one or two rooms to let, so it's important to book in advance during the summer season. More upmarket B&Bs, some in handsome period houses, have en suite bathrooms, free Wi-Fi and TVs in each room and usually charge from £35 per person per night.

Hostels

For those travelling on a tight budget, there is a network of hostels offering cheap accommodation in major cities, national parks and other areas of beauty, run by the Youth Hostel Association (YHA) ① *T01629-592600, or customer services T0800-0191 700,*

+44-1629-592700 from outside the UK, www.yha.org.uk. Membership costs from £14.35 a year and a bed in a dormitory costs from £15 to £25 a night. They offer bunk-bed accommodation in single-sex dormitories or smaller rooms, as well as family rooms, kitchen and laundry facilities. Though some rural hostels are still strict on discipline and impose a 2300 curfew, those in larger towns and cities tend to be more relaxed and doors are closed as late as 0200. Some larger hostels provide breakfasts for around £2.50 and three-course evening meals for £4-5. You should always phone ahead, as many hostels are closed during the day and phone numbers are listed in this guide. Advance booking is recommended at all times, particularly from May to September and on public holidays. Many hostels are closed during the winter. Youth hostel members are entitled to various discounts, including tourist attractions and travel. The YHA also offer budget self-catering bunkhouses with mostly dorm accommodation and some family rooms, which are in more rural locations. Camping barns, camping pods and camping are other options offered by the YHA; see the website for details.

Details of most independent hostels can be found in the *Independent Hostel Guide* (T01629-580427, www.independenthostelguide.co.uk). Independent hostels tend to be more laid-back, with fewer rules and no curfew, and no membership is required. They all have dorms, hot showers and self-catering kitchens, and some have family and double rooms. Some include continental breakfast, or offer cheap breakfasts.

Self-catering accommodation

There are lots of different types of accommodation to choose from, to suit all budgets, ranging from luxury lodges, castles and lighthouses to basic cottages. Expect to pay at least £200-400 per week for a two-bedroom cottage in the winter, rising to £400-1000 in the high season, or more if it's a particularly nice place. A good source of information on self-catering accommodation is the **VisitEngland** website, www.visitengland.com, and its *VisitEngland Self-catering 2013* guide, which lists many properties and is available to buy from any tourist office and many bookshops, but there are also dozens of excellent websites to browse. Amongst the best websites are: www.cottages4you.co.uk, www.ruralretreats.co.uk and www.ownersdirect.co.uk. If you want to tickle a trout or feed a pet lamb, **Farm Stay UK** (www.farmstay.co.uk) offer over a thousand good value rural places to stay around England, all clearly listed on a clickable map.

More interesting places to stay are offered by the **Landmark Trust** ① *T01628-825925, www.landmarktrust.org.uk*, who rent out renovated historic landmark buildings, from atmospheric castles to cottages, and the **National Trust** ① *T0844-800 2070, www.national trustcottages.co.uk*, who provide a wide variety of different accommodation on their estates. A reputable agent for self-catering cottages is **English Country Cottages** ① *T0845-268 0785, www.english-country-cottages.co.uk*.

Campsites

Campsites vary greatly in quality and level of facilities. Some sites are only open from April to October. See the following sites: www.pitchup.com; www.coolcamping.com, good for finding characterful sites that allow campfires; www.ukcampsite.co.uk, which is the most comprehensive service with thousands of sites, many with pictures and reviews from punters; and www.campingandcaravanningclub.co.uk. The **Forestry Commission** have campsites on their wooded estates, see www.campingintheforest.com.

Food and drink in England

Food

Only 30 years ago few would have thought to come to England for haute cuisine. Since the 1980s, though, the English have been determinedly shrugging off their reputation for over-boiled cabbage and watery beef. Now cookery shows such as *Masterchef* are the most popular on TV after the soaps, and thanks in part to the wave of celebrity chefs they have created, you can expect a generally high standard of competence in restaurant kitchens. Pub food has also been transformed in recent years, and now many of them offer ambitious lunchtime and supper menus in so-called gastro pubs.

Most parts of the country still boast regional specialities and thanks to the diversity of ethnic communities, restaurants offer food from all over the world. Enjoy Chinatowns and diverse styles of Asian cooking in the cities, or cosy up in a pub next to a roaring log fire to sample some home-cooked specialities such as Lancashire hotpot, black pudding, Scouse (Liverpool's potato stew), Bakewell pudding and mild Cheshire cheese. The Sunday roast is a fine English tradition, best served with Yorkshire puddings, while Afternoon Tea of jam and scones is ever popular.

The biggest problem with eating out is the limited serving hours in some pubs and hotels, particularly in more remote locations. Some establishments only serve food 1200-1430 for lunch and 1830-2130 for supper. In small places especially, it can be difficult finding food outside these enforced times. Restaurants, fast-food outlets and the many chic bistros and café-bars, which can be found not only in the main cities but increasingly in smaller towns, often serve food all day till 2100 or later. The latter often offer very good value and above-average quality fare.

Drink

Drinking is a national hobby and sometimes a dangerous one at that. **Real ale** – flat, brown beer known as bitter, made with hops – is the national drink, but now struggles to maintain its market share in the face of fierce competition from continental lagers and alcopops. Many small independent breweries are still up and running though, as well as microbreweries attached to individual pubs, which produce far superior ales. Local specialities include the creamy headed local bitters – John Smith and Theakstons. In many pubs the basic ales are chilled under gas pressure like lagers, but the best ales, such as those from the independents, are 'real ales', still fermenting in the cask and served cool but not chilled (around 12°C) under natural pressure from a handpump, electric pump or air pressure fount. **Cider** (fermented apple juice) is also experiencing a resurgence of interest and is a speciality of Somerset. English **wine** is also proving surprisingly resilient: generally it compares favourably with German varieties and many vineyards now offer continental-style sampling sessions.

The **pub** is still traditional place to enjoy a drink: the best are usually freehouses (not tied to a brewery) and feature real log fires in winter, flower-filled gardens for the summer (even in cities occasionally) and most importantly, thriving local custom. Many also offer characterful accommodation and restaurants serving high-quality fare. Pubs are prey to the same market forces as any other business, though, and many a delightful local has succumbed to exorbitant property prices or to the bland makeover favoured by the large chains. In 2012, pubs were closing at the rate of 12 a week due to the recession.

Essentials A-Z

Accident and emergency

For police, fire brigade, ambulance and, in certain areas, mountain rescue or coastguard, T999 or T112.

Disabled travellers

Wheelchair users, and blind or partially sighted people are automatically given 34-50% discount on train fares, and those with other disabilities are eligible for the Disabled Person's Railcard, which costs £20 per year and gives a third off most tickets. If you will need assistance at a railway station, call the train company that manages the station you're starting your journey from 24 hrs in advance. Disabled UK residents can apply to their local councils for a concessionary bus pass. National Express have a helpline for disabled passengers, T08717-818179, to plan journeys and arrange assistance. They also sell a discount coach card for £10 for people with disabilities.

The English Tourist Board website, www.visitengland.com, has information on the National Accessible Scheme (NAS) logos to help disabled travellers find the right accommodation for their needs, as well as details of walks that are possible with wheelchairs and the Shopmobility scheme. Many local tourist offices offer accessibility details for their area.

Useful organizations include:
Radar, T020-7250 3222, www.radar.org.uk. A good source of advice and information. It produces an annual National Key Scheme Guide and key for gaining access to over 9000 toilet facilities across the UK.
Tourism for all, T0845-124 9971, www.holidaycare.org.uk, www.tourismforall.org.uk. An excellent source of information about travel and for identifying accessible accommodation in the UK.

Electricity

The current in Britain is 240V AC. Plugs have 3 square pins and adapters are widely available.

Health

For minor accidents go to the nearest casualty department or an Accident and Emergency (A&E) Unit at a hospital. For other enquiries phone NHS Direct 24 hrs (T0845-4647) or visit an NHS walk-in centre. See also individual town and city directories throughout the book for details of local medical services.

Money → *For up-to-date exchange rates, see www.xe.com.*

The British currency is the pound sterling (£), divided into 100 pence (p). Coins come in denominations of 1p, 2p, 5p, 10p, 20p, 50p, £1 and £2. Banknotes come in denominations of £5, £10, £20 and £50. The last of these is not widely used and may be difficult to change.

Banks and bureaux de change

Banks tend to offer similar exchange rates and are usually the best places to change money and cheques. Outside banking hours you'll have to use a bureau de change, which can be easily found at the airports and train stations and in larger cities. **Thomas Cook** and other major travel agents also operate bureaux de change with reasonable rates. Avoid changing money or cheques in hotels, as the rates are usually poor. Main post offices and branches of **Marks and Spencer** will change cash without charging commission.

Credit cards and ATMs

Most hotels, shops and restaurants accept the major credit cards though some places may charge for using them. Some smaller establishments such as B&Bs may only accept cash.

Currency cards

If you don't want to carry lots of cash, prepaid currency cards allow you to preload money from your bank account, fixed at the day's exchange rate. They look like a credit or debit card and are issued by specialist money changing companies, such as **Travelex** and **Caxton FX**. You can top up and check your balance by phone, online and sometimes by text.

Money transfers

If you need money urgently, the quickest way to have it sent to you is to have it wired to the nearest bank via **Western Union**, T0800-833 833, www.westernunion.co.uk, or **MoneyGram**, www.moneygram.com. The Post Office can also arrange a MoneyGram transfer. Charges are on a sliding scale; so it will cost proportionately less to wire out more money. Money can also be wired by **Thomas Cook**, www.thomasexchangeglobal.co.uk, or transferred via a bank draft, but this can take up to a week.

Taxes

Most goods are subject to a Value Added Tax (VAT) of 20%, with the major exception of food and books. VAT is usually already included in the advertised price of goods. Visitors from non-EU countries can save money through shopping at places that offer Tax Free Shopping (also known as the Retail Export Scheme), which allows a refund of VAT on goods that will be taken out of the country. Note that not all shops participate in the scheme and that VAT cannot be reclaimed on hotel bills or other services.

Cost of travelling

England can be an expensive place to visit, and London and the south in particular can eat heavily into your budget. There is budget accommodation available, however, and backpackers will be able to keep their costs down. Fuel is a major expense and won't just cost an arm and a leg but also the limbs of all remaining family members, and public transport – particularly rail travel if not booked in advance – can also be pricey, especially for families. Accommodation and restaurant prices also tend to be higher in more popular destinations and during the busy summer months.

The minimum daily budget required, if you're staying in hostels or camping, cycling or hitching (not recommended), and cooking your own meals, will be around £30 per person per day. If you start using public transport and eating out occasionally that will rise to around £35-40. Those staying in slightly more upmarket B&Bs or guesthouses, eating out every evening at pubs or modest restaurants and visiting tourist attractions can expect to pay around £60 per day. If you also want to hire a car and eat well, then costs will rise considerably to at least £75-80 per person per day. Single travellers will have to pay more than half the cost of a double room, and should budget on spending around 60-70% of what a couple would spend.

Opening hours

Businesses are usually open Mon-Sat 0900-1700. In towns and cities, as well as villages in holiday areas, many shops open on a Sun but they will open later and close earlier. For banks, see above. For TIC opening hours, see the tourist information sections in the relevant cities, towns and villages in the text.

Post

Most post offices are open Mon-Fri 0900 to 1730 and Sat 0900-1230 or 1300. Smaller sub-post offices are closed for an hour at lunch (1300-1400) and many of them operate out of a shop. Stamps can be bought at post offices, but also from many shops. A 1st-class letter weighing up to 100 g to anywhere in the UK costs 60p (a large letter over 240 mm by 165 mm is 90p) and should arrive the following day, while 2nd-class letters weighing up to 100 g cost 50p (69p) and take between 2-4 days. For more information about Royal Mail postal services, call T08457-740740, or visit www.royalmail.com.

Safety
Generally speaking, England is a safe place to visit. English cities have their fair share of crime, but much of it is drug-related and confined to the more deprived peripheral areas. Trust your instincts, and if in doubt, take a taxi.

Telephone → *Country code +44.*
Useful numbers: operator T100; international operator T155; directory enquiries T192; overseas directory enquiries T153.
Most public payphones are operated by British Telecom (**BT**) and can be found in towns and cities, though less so in rural areas. Numbers of public phone booths have declined in recent years due to the ubiquity of the mobile phone, so don't rely on being able to find a payphone wherever you go. Calls from BT payphones cost a minimum of 60p, for which you get 30 mins for a local or national call. Calls to non-geographic numbers (eg 0845), mobile phones and others may cost more. Payphones take either coins (10p, 20p, 50p and £1), 50c, 1 or 2 euro coins, credit cards or BT Chargecards, which are available at newsagents and post offices displaying the BT logo. These cards come in denominations of £2, £3, £5 and £10. Some payphones also have facilities for internet, text messaging and emailing.

For most countries (including Europe, USA and Canada) calls are cheapest Mon-Fri between 1800 and 0800 and all day Sat-Sun. For Australia and New Zealand it's cheapest to call from 1430-1930 and from 2400-0700 every day. However, the cheapest ways to call abroad from England is not via a standard UK landline provider. Calls are free

using **Skype** on the internet, or you can route calls from your phone through the internet with **JaJah** (www.jajah.com) or from a mobile using **Rebtel**. Many phone companies offer discounted call rates by calling their access number prior to dialling the number you want, including www.dialabroad.co.uk and www.simply-call.com.

Area codes are not needed if calling from within the same area. Any number prefixed by 0800 or 0500 is free to the caller; 08457 numbers are charged at local rates and 08705 numbers at the national rate.

Time
Greenwich Mean Time (GMT) is used from late Oct to late Mar, after which time the clocks go forward 1 hr to British Summer Time (BST).

Tipping
Tipping in England is at the customer's discretion. In a restaurant you should leave a tip of 10-15% if you are satisfied with the service. If the bill already includes a service charge, which is likely if you are in a large group, you needn't add a further tip. Tipping is not normal in pubs or bars. Taxi drivers may expect a tip for longer journeys, usually around 10%.

Tourist information
Tourist information centres (TICs) can be found in most towns. Their addresses, phone numbers and opening hours are listed in the relevant sections of this book. Opening hours vary depending on the time of year, and many of the smaller offices are closed or have limited opening hours during the winter months. All tourist offices provide information on accommodation, public transport, local attractions and restaurants, as well as selling books, local guides, maps and souvenirs. Many also have free street plans and leaflets describing local walks. They can also book accommodation for a small fee.

Museums, galleries and historic houses

Over 300 stately homes, gardens and countryside areas, are cared for by the **National Trust** (**NT**), T0844-800 1895, www.nationaltrust.org.uk. If you're going to be visiting several sights during your stay, then it's worth taking annual membership, which costs £53, £25 if you're aged under 26 and £70 for a family, giving free access to all National Trust properties. A similar organization is **English Heritage** (**EH**), T0870-333 1181, www.english-heritage.org.uk, which manages hundreds of ancient monuments and other sights around England, including Stonehenge, and focuses on restoration and preservation. Membership includes free admission to sites, and advance information on events, and costs £47 per adult to £82 per couple, under-19s free. **Natural England**, T0845-600 3078, www.naturalengland.org.uk, is concerned with restoring and conserving the English countryside, and can give information on walks and events in the countryside.

Many other historic buildings are owned by local authorities, and admission is cheap, or in many cases free. Most municipal art galleries and museums are free, as well as most state-owned museums, particularly those in London and other large cities. Most fee-paying attractions give a discount or concession for senior citizens, the unemployed, full-time students and children under 16 (those under 5 are admitted free in most places). Proof of age or status must be shown.

Finding out more

The best way of finding out more information is to contact Visit England (aka the English Tourist Board), www.visitengland.com. Alternatively, you can contact VisitBritain, the organization responsible for tourism. Both organizations can provide a wealth of free literature and information such as maps, city guides and accommodation brochures.

Travellers with special needs should also contact VisitEngland or their nearest VisitBritain office. If you want more detailed information on a particular area, contact the specific tourist boards; see in the main text for details.

Visas and immigration

Visa regulations are subject to change, so it is essential to check with your local British embassy, high commission or consulate before leaving home. Citizens of all European countries – except Albania, Bosnia Herzegovina, Kosovo, Macedonia, Moldova, Turkey, Serbia and all former Soviet republics (other than the Baltic states) – require only a passport to enter Britain and can generally stay for up to 3 months. Citizens of Australia, Canada, New Zealand, South Africa or the USA can stay for up to 6 months, providing they have a return ticket and sufficient funds to cover their stay. Citizens of most other countries require a visa from the commission or consular office in the country of application.

The UK Border Agency, www.ukba. homeoffice.gov.uk, is responsible for UK immigration matters and its website is a good place to start for anyone hoping visit, work, study or emigrate to the UK. For visa extensions also contact the UK Border Agency via the website. Citizens of Australia, Canada, New Zealand, South Africa or the USA wishing to stay longer than 6 months will need an Entry Clearance Certificate from the British High Commission in their country. For more details, contact your nearest British embassy, consulate or high commission, or the Foreign and Commonwealth Office in London.

Weights and measures

Imperial and metric systems are both in use. Distances on roads are measured in miles and yards, drinks poured in pints and gills, but generally, the metric system is used elsewhere.

Contents

Footprint features

Northwest England

Manchester

Manchester, said French footballer Eric Cantona, is a city in love with "le football, la fête et la musique." Many things have changed since the mid-1990s when he played for Manchester United, but the city still prays to that holy trinity of sport, partying and music. Manchester was at the forefront of the industrial revolution of the 18th and 19th centuries, but that image is receding fast. The Commonwealth Games of 2002 brought a huge influx of money and allowed Manchester to transform itself into the city it is today; the Victorian workhouses are now being celebrated for their architecture and have been redeveloped into luxury flats, offices and nightclubs.

Urbis, the world's first museum about city life, and the Imperial War Museum North are two exceptionally confrontational glass and steel structures that shape the city like the Guggenheim has Bilbao. There's stiff competition from Leeds and Liverpool for the title of best clubbing town in England, but Manchester's just got the edge over its rivals with three universities and a thriving gay scene. Manchester's a warm-hearted, fast-moving city with history, humour and high-spirits running in its veins. But whatever you're doing, make sure you do it with a pint of locally brewed Boddington's in your hand – lager is for southerners.

Arriving in Manchester → *For listings, see pages 28-34.*

Getting there

Air Manchester Airport ① *T08712-710711, www.manchesterairport.co.uk*, is 12 miles south of the city and is the largest airport outside of London. As well as international flights, there are connections from 17 airports within the UK. There are ATMs, bureaux de change, car hire desks and free Wi-Fi in all three terminals, as well as two **tourist information centres** ① *Terminal 1, T0161-436 3344, Mon-Fri 0800-2100, Sat and Sun 0800-1800; Terminal 2, T0161-489 6412, daily 0730-1230*, which can book accommodation and coach tickets. The airport's integrated transport hub, **The Station**, is where local and long-distance transport arrives and departs. Trains to the city centre run every 10 minutes into Piccadilly train station (£4.70); the average journey time is 20 minutes. Buses also run to and from the city 24 hours a day. Suggested taxi companies from the airport include: Arrow Cars, T0161-489 8899, a private company located at each terminal; and **Hackney Cabs**, which pick up outside each of the terminals. The journey to the costs about £24.

Bus The main bus station is on Chorlton Street for all regional and national buses. **National Express** ① *T08705-808080, www.nationalexpress.co.uk*, runs coaches from most major towns and cities including London (4¾ hours, hourly) and Liverpool (1 hour 20 minutes, hourly).

Car The M62 connects Manchester with Leeds and the Humber region to the east and Liverpool to the west. The M6 takes you to Manchester from Birmingham in the south and Scotland in the north; the M56 links the city with North Wales and Chester. It takes 3½ hours to get to Manchester from London and Glasgow, three hours from Cardiff and Edinburgh, and 1½ hours from Birmingham.

Train Manchester Piccadilly in the city centre is the main station for national and regional rail services. There are direct connections with London Euston (three hours, seven daily), Liverpool Lime Street (45 minutes, every 30 minutes), Blackpool (1¼ hours, every 30 minutes) and Newcastle (three hours, six daily). For the cheapest tickets visit www.thetrainline.co.uk. ▶ *See Transport, page 36.*

Getting around

Despite being one of England's major cities, Manchester's city centre is compact and you can walk it in about 20 minutes. The city is split into eight village-like districts, which merge into one, so you can easily wander around them in an afternoon.

The city's tram system, **Metrolink** ① *www.metrolink.co.uk*, is a good way to get around the central district. Trams were brought back to Manchester about 20 years ago and are reliable and clean, unlike the buses. This tram network stretches from Bury to Altrincham and out to Eccles. Tickets can be bought from machines on the platforms and trams run every 12 minutes. A return ticket from Piccadilly to Salford Quays costs £2.90.

The **Metroshuttle** ① *TFGM, T0161-244 1000, www.tfgm.com*, is a free shuttlebus service that links all the main car parks, stations and tram stops around the city centre's main attractions. Buses operate Monday to Saturday 0700-1900, Sunday 1000-1800 every 10 minutes and more frequently during rush-hour. The No 1 goes to Victoria Station (for the MEN arena and Urbis) via Chinatown and Kendals department store on Deansgate before heading back to Piccadilly; the No 2 takes you down to Oxford Road and Deansgate stations via the Town Hall and then back to Piccadilly.

Day Saver tickets, allowing unlimited travel on local bus, train and Metrolink services, cost £11. For details contact **Transport For Greater Manchester (TFGM)** ① *2 Piccadilly Place, T0161-244 1000, www.tfgm.com, Mon-Fri 0900-1700*, or **Traveline** ① *T0871-200 2233, www.traveline.info*.

Orientation
Beside Piccadilly station is the bohemian Northern Quarter. Across the road from Piccadilly station running mainly along Canal Street is the Gay Village. The centre of Manchester, just off St Peter's Square, has Chinatown. Peter's Fields is the main business and conference area, also containing the Bridgewater Hall, the city's premier classical music venue. Manchester University is mainly on Oxford Road. Castlefield to the southwest sits on the canal network. Deansgate Locks, just a totter in high heels away, is also on the canal network. Up by Victoria station in the north is the Millennium Quarter, redeveloped since the IRA bomb of 1996. Rusholme, the Indian district in the south of Manchester, is also known as 'the curry mile'. Just out of Manchester to the southwest is Salford Quays, the old industrial port area which has also been redeveloped. The home of Manchester United, Old Trafford, is just across the Manchester Ship Canal from here, and here you'll also find the Imperial War Museum of the North and The Lowry, an art gallery, theatre, cinema and discount shopping outlet.

Tourist information
Manchester Visitor Information Centre ① *Piccadilly Plaza, Portland St, T0871-222 8223, www.visitmanchester.com, Mon-Sat 0930-1730, Sun 1030-1630*, arranges accommodation, city walking tours, theatre and coach tickets, and car hire. **Salford Quays TIC** ① *1 The Quays, T0161-848 8601, Mon-Sat 0830-1630, Sun 1000-1600*, provides information about Old Trafford, The Lowry and the Imperial War Museum of the North.

The websites www.destinationmanchester.com and www.manchester.com have useful up-to-date listings about the area. Your best bet if you've come to Manchester for a short break is to pick up a copy of *CityLife*, www.citylife.co.uk, the city's glossy listings magazine. It's published fortnightly on a Tuesday and is good for all things young, fun and Mancunian. The *Manchester Evening News* is the regional daily newspaper with listings, and *The Metro* is a free daily commuter paper with digested national news and local listings.

Background

Manchester's past is perhaps not as bright as its future. The town takes its name from the oldest part of its history, the turf and timber Roman fort of Mamucium established in AD 79 in the area now called Castlefield. Somewhat overshadowed, it was used as an intermediate port between the more important towns of York, Chester and Buxton.

The city had to wait a long time before it came to prominence. It expanded considerably as a market town in the 18th century with the addition of the Bridgewater canal, which connected the town with much of Cheshire, and things began to look up. This canal infrastructure was instrumental in the creation of the Cottonopolis, the name given to Manchester as it became the cotton capital of the world and one of Britain's

24-hour party people

If you've only got 24 hours to spend in Manchester, use it well to soak up the culture of the city – but bring an umbrella, as the city has a reputation as one of the wettest in England.

Start your day with a designer coffee in the Triangle centre in the Millennium Quarter before moving on to take in the independent record shops and boutiques of the Northern Quarter. Have lunch in a bar on Oldham Street then jump on the Metrolink and get out to Salford Quays for the afternoon. Make the most of the Imperial War Museum of the North and The Lowry art gallery here, two of Manchester's most dazzling museums, which display different aspects of this diverse city. A curry in Rusholme should see you right for dinner so you can then head towards Deansgate Locks for a beer or two before going clubbing in one of the many waterside bars. Have a kebab and wave to the milkman on the way home.

leading industrial cities. Located on the River Irwell and close to the ports of Liverpool and Chester, the city was perfectly situated to take advantage of developments in textile manufacture. Mills sprang up everywhere and were surrounded by cheap terraced housing as depicted in the paintings of Salford-born LS Lowry.

This new-found sense of purpose came at a price though. The population of 76,000 in 1801 had grown to 316,000 by 1851, and it isn't hard to imagine the strain that this put on the city. (While working in his father's factory, a young Frederick Engels was one of many writers who criticized the working conditions of Manchester.) The rapid industrialization led to social and political unrest. On 16 August 1819, 11 people were killed and a total of 400 wounded when 50,000 people turned out for a meeting held in St Peter's Field in support of parliamentary reform for factory workers' conditions. The disaster is known as the Peterloo Massacre, but it still took 13 long years for the parliamentary reform act of 1832 to consider representing and supporting the underclasses. By the time that Manchester City Council was established in 1853 to deal with the city's economic and social problems, the mills were in decline. Manchester was under threat from cheaper manufacturers abroad, and by 1870 German and American factories were more competitive. Consequently, slum areas persisted, and the city suffered a great depression.

The Second World War also brought immense destruction to Manchester, particularly in December 1940 when the Christmas blitz decimated the city and some 30,000 houses were damaged. It was almost a blessing in disguise though, as the rebuilding programme eliminated the slum housing and established municipal housing areas. (Not entirely successfully in areas such as Moss Side, which became synonymous with violence and crime.)

In 1996, destruction came in the form of an IRA bomb which disabled Market Street and principally the Arndale Centre, in an attack that cost millions to rectify. Still, it wasn't all in vain: it allowed Marks and Spencer to rebuild their Market Street store as the biggest in the world. Hosting the Commonwealth Games in 2002 prompted an almost entire redevelopment of the Piccadilly and Salford Quays areas and the creation of sprightly new attractions, including The Paintworks, the Triangle and URBIS. Today the city has Britain's third-largest urban economy with two universities, as well as two premier league football teams, and it is now the proud host of the nation's first and only National Football Museum.

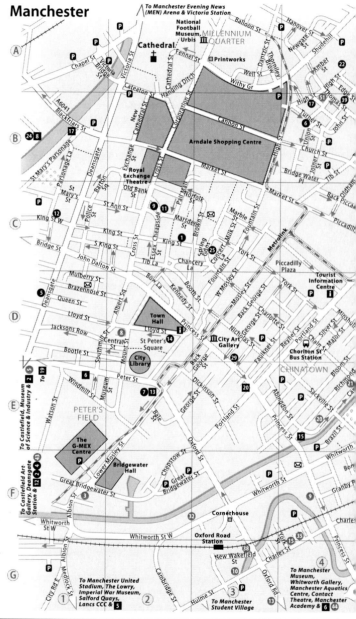

Manchester

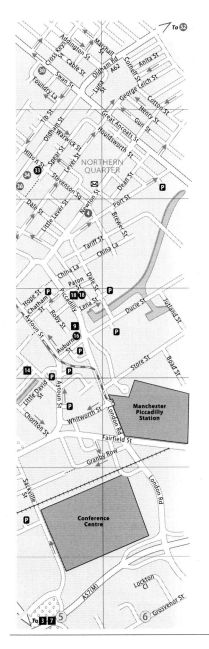

N

100 metres
100 yards

Where to stay
Abode **18** *D5*
Eleven Didsbury
  Park **3** *G5*
Etrop Grange **5** *G1*
Great John Street **2** *E1*
The Lowry **8** *B1*
Malmaison
  Manchester **9** *D5*
Manchester YHA **12** *F1*
Midland **13** *E2*
New Union **15** *E4*
Radisson Edwardian **6** *E1*
Renaissance **17** *B1*
Velvet **14** *D5*
Victoria Warehouse **19** *E1*
Roomzzz
  Aparthotel **20** *E3*

Restaurants
39 Steps **1** *C2*
Atlas **2** *F1*
Australasia **5** *D1*
Chaophraya **11** *C2*
Dimitri's **4** *F1*
Earth Vegetarian
  Café **6** *B4*
French Restaurant **7** *E2*
Grinch **9** *C2*
Koreana **12** *C1*
Livebait **14** *D2*
Malmaison
  Brasserie **16** *D5*
Market **17** *B4*

Northern Quarter **22** *A4*
On the Eighth Day **19** *G4*
Michael Caines
  @ Abode **18** *D5*
River Bar
  & Restaurant **24** *B1*
Rosso **25** *C3*
Soup Kitchen **33** *B5*
Teacup Café **39** *B4*
Yang Sing **29** *D3*

Pubs, bars & clubs
The Band on the
  Wall **30** *A5*
Britons Protection
  League **3** *F1*
Citrus Bar **8** *D2*
Cloud 23 **43** *F1*
Cornerhouse **32** *F3*
Dry **34** *B5*
Factory 251 **9** *F4*
Font Bar **10** *G3*
Lass O'Gowrie **35** *F4*
Night & Day
  Café **36** *B5*
Odd Bar **51** *B4*
Odder Bar **13** *G3*
Po Na Na Souk Bar **15** *G4*
Revolution **38** *G3*
Sankeys **52** *A6*
Tribeca BED Bar **20** *E4*
Trof **44** *G4*
Via **21** *E4*

Places in Manchester

Salford Quays

Not so long ago, the Quays area was a bit shabby and run-down, a relic of the industrial period that was still in use and that you'd only recommend visiting to your worst enemy. Now, though, it's the place to be seen, with an art gallery and museum that have been instrumental in Manchester's reinvention as a city of dynamism and culture. It's also spitting distance from Manchester's main claim to fame, the home turf of Manchester United at Old Trafford. Salford Quays is about a mile and a half to the southwest of the city centre and easily reached by Metrolink from Harbour City and Old Trafford tram stops.

Tickets to see Man United play are like gold dust even if you are a member, but you can console yourself with a look round the changing rooms and down on to the pitch at the **Manchester United Museum and Tour** ① *North Stand, Old Trafford, Sir Matt Busby Way, T0161-868 8000 www.manutd.com, daily 0930-1700, closed on match days and the day before champions' league games, museum and tour £16, concessions £10.50.* There's a lot to see here, from Busby's babes to glittering trophies, Best, Beckham and boots and plenty of stats and history for the die-hard fan.

Just one stop away on the Metrolink will take you to Harbour City and the Quays itself. It's a tough call, but of the two museums here, **The Lowry** ① *Pier 8, T0843-208 6000, www.thelowry.com, Tue-Fri 1100-2000, Sat 1000-2000, Sun-Mon 1100-1800, free except for special exhibitions,* is probably the best, although you can easily visit this and the Imperial War Museum of the North (see below) in an afternoon. Salford's most illustrious son painted scenes of Manchester and the surrounding area in the first half of the 20th century, and his depiction of workers with eyes red-rimmed from the dust, and malnourished children speak more about the city than any of the museums. He's most famous for his paintings of stick people pouring into the factory gates, but while there are a number of them on display, the individual portraits show another side to him, as do his views across the city to the Peak District. The Lowry exhibition is permanent, and there are also rotating exhibitions by local and national artists, two theatres, a café, a restaurant and beautiful views across the quays.

Across the bridge from The Lowry you can see the stunning **Imperial War Museum of the North** ① *Trafford Wharf, T0161-836 4000, www.iwm.org.uk, daily 1000-1700, free,* arcing across the sky. The building itself, designed by the architect Daniel Libeskind and opened in 2002, is as much a draw as what's inside. He decided to represent conflict on the three planes of

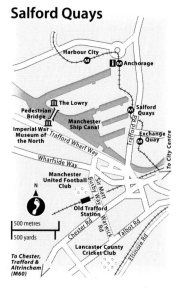

Salford Quays

air, water and land with the three shards of glass and steel which divide your view here, and it certainly works as a confrontational structure. Manchester was decimated by bombs in the Second World War and, with the Imperial War Museum miles away in London, it's been a long-standing travesty that those in the north couldn't access this part of the nation's history, but now it's the Londoners who will feel left out. The focus of the museum is on the way that war shapes people's lives over a variety of different conflict situations, and it contains thought-provoking and state-of-the-art exhibits.

St Peter's Square and around

On the west side of the square are the **Town Hall** and **Manchester City Library** ① *Elliot House, 141 Deansgate, T0161-234 1983, Mon-Thu 0900-2000, Fri-Sat 0900-1700*. The Town Hall is one of the city's original Victorian buildings with a clear connection to the Cottonopolis days. It was built in the style of a medieval Flemish cloth hall, which gives the square a European feel, and has murals inside it by Ford Madox Brown. Manchester Library is the central library for the university and the city's other citizens and has a beautiful frescoed ceiling inside as well as archives for Manchester and an extensive music library.

Across the road on Mosley Street is the **City Art Gallery** ① *T0161-235 8888, www.manchestergalleries.org, Tue-Sun 1000-1700, free*, which shows a wide variety of art from the Pre-Raphaelites to the Renaissance, Turner, Constable and a range of 20th-century art. The gallery seems to go on forever and has an unmissable interactive gallery where you can learn about inspirations for paintings.

Oxford Road and around

To the north of the square, Peter Street running alongside the Library turns into Oxford Road. This is the main student area in Manchester and consequently has some good bars and clubs as well as a number of art galleries and university facilities. Oxford Road station is the main access point for this area if you don't fancy a walk, but it's not far from St Peter's Square at all. All buses except the No 47 will take you down Oxford Road.

Just outside the station is the avant-garde **Cornerhouse** ① *70 Oxford Rd, T0161-228 7621, www.cornerhouse.org, galleries Tue-Sat 1200-2000, Sun 1200-1800, closed Mon, free*, containing three galleries, three cinemas, two cafés, a bookshop and a bar. It's just about the best place in Manchester for foreign cinema and has varied exhibitions of modern art. The bar looks out on to Oxford Road and serves a host of foreign bottled beers for you to swig while watching passers-by. For cinema, see page 34.

Further down Oxford Road is **Manchester Museum** ① *T0161-275 2648, www.museum.manchester.ac.uk, Tue-Sat 1000-1700, Sun-Mon 1100-1600, free, virtually every bus going in this direction goes past it*, at the University of Manchester. It's a traditional museum that's good for children, with its anthropological and natural history exhibits and gallery of live frogs, lizards and snakes. Manchester doesn't have a zoo, so this is the next best thing. There's also a range of well-preserved mummies.

Opposite the Manchester Royal Infirmary you'll find the city's most traditional art gallery, the **Whitworth Art Gallery** ① *10 mins further down Oxford Rd from Manchester Museum, but it's too far to walk so take the bus, T0161-275 7450, www.whitworth. manchester.ac.uk, Mon-Sat 1000-1700, Sun 1200-1600, free*. Founded in 1889, it's the university's art gallery and specializes in watercolours, textiles and wallpaper. It also has a large collection of Turners and, as you will come to expect from a quick tour of Manchester's galleries, there's some modern art and sculpture in there too.

Castlefield

Castlefield, the oldest part of Manchester, has a couple of exceptional older museums that are particularly family-friendly, but after dark it's one of the main party areas, with classy bars overlooking the canals. The Roman fort of Mamucium was situated here 2000 years ago, and in later years the canals and railways helped to drive the industrial revolution. It became Britain's first urban heritage park in the 1980s and retains many original Victorian buildings including an 1830s warehouse down towards the river. Take the train to Deansgate station and then take a left to find Castlefield; otherwise try the GMEX Metrolink stop.

It's no surprise given this area's industrial heritage that the **Museum of Science and Industry** ① *Liverpool Rd, T0161-832 2244, www.mosi.org.uk, daily 1000-1700, free, turn left out of Deansgate station*, is here, housed partly in old Victorian buildings. It tells of Manchester's industrial history and even offers you the chance to smell the Victorian sewers, reconstructed of course. Look out for the excellent air and space gallery with a host of aviational and astronomical models and interactive features. Big budget scientific exhibitions change regularly, and there's often a surcharge to enter them.

Around the corner on Bridge Street, the **People's History Museum** ① *T0161-838 9190, www.phm.org.uk, daily 1000-1700, free*, reopened its doors in 2010 after a £12.5 million makeover. Fused to the Grade II-listed pumphouse is a brand new wing and café which give the place a light, airy feel. Mancunians are rightly proud of their history, and the museum tells the story of the ordinary people involved in industry from the beginning right through to today, including the rise of trade unions and the Suffragette movement which began close by in Lancashire. There are a lot of trade union banners, and it's an interesting look at how England's social fabric has developed over the years.

Closer to the station in Knott Mill is **Castlefield Art Gallery** ① *2 Hewitt St, T0161-832 8034, www.castlefieldgallery.co.uk, galleries Wed-Sun 1300-1800, free*, Manchester's leading left-of-field art space – and that's saying something – with very modern and challenging exhibitions.

Northern Quarter

With no real sights to speak of, the Northern Quarter, the area between Piccadilly and Ancoats, is the hippest part of town and the heart of urban creativity in the city. With countless independent record shops, cafés, bars, restaurants and fashion stores, including the world-famous shopping emporium **Afflecks**, the area has seen massive regeneration in recent years and retains a unique character and charm. For information on what's going on in this part of town, visit http://northernquartermanchester.com.

Millennium Quarter

Up in the north of the city is the newly named Millennium Quarter, a substantially redeveloped area around Victoria station, reachable by train and Metrolink. The first thing you'll see as you pitch up at the station is the massive **Manchester Evening News (MEN) Arena**, a huge stadium that hosts all manner of things from Manchester Storm ice hockey team on a Sunday to touring rock and pop acts. Directly across from this is **Chetham's**,

Humble beginnings

The Red Devils have a history of flamboyant players from George Best to clothes horse and media icon David Beckham. It wasn't always this way, though, as they started out in 1878 as a local works football team, Newton Heath Lancashire and Yorkshire Railway. They joined the fledgling football league in 1892 and soon ran into financial difficulty. But a chance encounter by the captain's dog and local brewery owner John Henry Davies found a saviour for the soon-to-be red devils. He invested in the club, and in 1902 they were renamed Manchester United. A move to Old Trafford in 1910, owned by Davies's Manchester Brewery Company, came not a minute too soon. Two days previously the old wooden Bank Street stand blew over in high winds. It was a good omen for the club as, by the end of their first full season at Old Trafford, Manchester United were the new league champions.

Manchester's top classical music academy, and the **Urbis Building**. This immense £30 million 'glass-skinned' building caused controversy in the city when it was built as another of the bright, new attractions for the 2002 Commonwealth Games. It's all about urban living, something that Manchester knows a lot about, and looks broadly at how the concept has developed through other countries and scenarios. The self-conscious modernity of the building is its real draw though, with a great glass elevator and exhibits that don't just involve you but use your participation to continually develop the way that it portrays city life.

The Urbis now has another raison d'être as the home of the **National Football Museum** ① *Cathedral Gardens, T0161-605 8200, www.nationalfootballmuseum.com, Mon-Sat 1000-1700, Sun 1100-1700, free*. The world's biggest and best football museum opened its doors in 2012 and brings to life the story of 'the people's game' through a range of interactive and hands-on displays. The museum explores how football has impacted on English society and culture over the past 150 years and developed into the a worldwide obsession. It aims to preserve, conserve and interpret important collections of football memorabilia, including the ball from the 1966 World Cup final, Diego Maradona's famous 'Hand of God' shirt and the very first hand-written rule book. You can even try your luck in the Football Plus (£2.50), a series of interactive stations that allow you to test your skills in simulated conditions. It's not just for football fans.

Manchester listings

For hotel and restaurant price codes and other relevant information, see pages 9-12.

🛏 Where to stay

Manchester *p18, map p22*
The visitor information centre (see page 20) has further information on B&Bs in and around Manchester. Accommodation in the centre of Manchester is expensive and generally business-orientated. There are a few nice retreats, though, and down Canal St are a couple of characterful gay hotels. The YHA is very good but expensive, and your best bet for B&Bs is to look a little further out of town on Oxford Rd. Make sure that you get in early with your bookings, though, as when Manchester United are at home there's scarcely a bed to be found.

£££ Great John Street Hotel, Great John St, T0161-831 3211, www.eclectichotels.co.uk/ great-john-street. A Victorian schoolhouse converted into a boutique townhouse hotel with rooftop bar and hot tub, well located for the shops and theatres. Stylish bedrooms.

£££ The Lowry Hotel, 50 Dearman's Pl, Chapel Wharf, T0161-827 8883, www.the lowryhotel.com. Manchester's first 5-star hotel remains the most exclusive place to stay with a great location next to the river. It offers everything you'd expect of a top modern hotel, including **River Restaurant**, spa and leisure facilities. It even organizes shopping and spa breaks; you'll be seriously pampered.

£££ Malmaison Manchester, Gore St, T0845-365 4247, www.malmaison.com/ locations/manchester. Right in the middle of the not-so-exclusive Piccadilly area, opposite the station, this is a seriously chic, light and airy place to stay. Minimalist without being distant or pretentious. There's a gym, spa and brasserie, and the additional attraction of a CD library for guests.

£££ The Midland Hotel, 16 Peter St, T0161-236 3333, www.qhotels.co.uk. This stately Edwardian hotel is one of the most imposing buildings in the city. Decorative marbled halls, huge 4-poster beds, a gym and an excellent French restaurant are some of the attractions. It's seen some rock stars in its time and is the height of luxury.

£££ Radisson Blue Edwardian Hotel, Free Trade Hall, Peter St, T0800-374411, www.radissonblu-edwardian.com/ manchester. 5-star luxury in a historic building opposite Bridgwater Hall. Rooms have king-sized beds, slate bathrooms and walk-in wardrobes. Free Wi-Fi, 12-m pool, hot tub and **Siena** spa. The **Opus One** restaurant offers fine dining while the **Alto** is more relaxed.

£££ Velvet, 2 Canal St, T0161-236 9003, www.velvetmanchester.com. A chic and stylish hotel on one of Manchester's most famous streets. Beautiful rooms with elegant decor including iPod dock, Wi-Fi and luxury bathrobes. The **Velvet Lounge Bar** has live DJs on weekends and a fish tank in the stairs.

££ ABode Manchester, 107 Piccadilly, T0161-247 7744, www.abodehotels.co.uk/ manchester. Funky central hotel with a young hip vibe. Set in a Grade II listed building, this former cotton merchant warehouse retains its period features and offers 21 stylish rooms and 5-loft-style suites. Notable for its **Michael Caines** restaurant (see Restaurants, below), there's also an Italian café/restaurant and a jazz lounge downstairs.

££ The Castlefield Hotel, Liverpool Rd, T0161-832 7073, www.castlefield-hotel.co.uk. A classy modern hotel with a restaurant, bar and gym and friendly staff all overlooking the canal. There's even a running track underneath the hotel, alongside basketball and squash courts and a swimming pool, making it one of the largest gyms in the Northwest.

££ Ox Hotel, 71 Liverpool Rd, Castlefield, T0161 839 7760, http://theox.co.uk. Recently refurbished, this historic pub offers spacious en suite rooms with Wi-Fi opposite the Museum of Science and Industry.

££ Renaissance Manchester City Centre Hotel, Blackfriars St, T0161-831 6000, www.marriott.co.uk/hotels/travel/manbr-renaissance-manchester-city-centre-hotel. Large luxury modern hotel as close as you can get to the best of Manchester's cultural attractions such as the Royal Exchange, the MEN arena and Salford Quays, not to mention restaurants and shopping areas.

££-£ Elton Bank Hotel, 62 Platt Lane, Rusholme, T0161-225 3388, www.eltonbankhotel.com. A small and friendly family-run hotel by the University sports grounds. Fairly basic accommodation but not far from the city centre as well as the Indian and Middle-Eastern delights of Rusholme itself.

££-£ Victoria Warehouse Hotel, Trafford Rd, southwest of the centre, T0161-660 7000, www.victoriawarehouse.com. Rustic urban hotel full of character and a chilled out indie vibe. As well as a bistro, mini movie theatre, library and lounge, there's a yoga centre and spa. Rooms are en suite with flatscreen TV.

£ Little Northern Hotel, 67 Thomas St, T0161-839 0213, www.littlenorthern hotel.co.uk. A coaching inn dating back to 1700 above **The Millstone** pub. It's recently been refurbished and is a bargain price for its location in the heart of the shabby-retro-chic of the Northern Quarter. Expect standard pub/B&B treatment and a number of locals sitting in the corner of the bar.

£ Manchester YHA, Potato Wharf, 5 mins from Deansgate train station, T0845-371 9647, www.yha.org.uk/hostel/manchester. Accommodation here isn't all that cheap, but you get what you pay for. Light, airy, clean and spacious, this newish big hostel is right on the canalside in Castlefield and staff are really friendly. Breakfast included in the price.

£ The New Union Hotel, at the junction of Princess St and Canal St, T0161-228 1492, www.newunionhotel.com. Not posh or classy, but a gay-friendly hotel with plenty of atmosphere and loud blaring music. A good value option; and they serve breakfast on your return from your all-night partying.

Manchester suburbs

£££ Eleven Didsbury Park, 11 Didsbury Park, Didsbury Village, T0161-448 7711, www.elevendidsburypark.com. A classic contemporary townhouse hotel with minimalist design, polished floorboards and funky armchairs. A little different from staying in the beating heart of town but without compromising the style.

£££-££ Didsbury House Hotel, Didsbury Park, T0161-448 2200, www.eclectichotels.co.uk/didsbury-house. Run by the same people as 11 Didsbury Park, this luxury Victorian townhouse has a guest lounge and bar as well as 20 individually styled bedrooms. A chic urban retreat.

£££-££ Etrop Grange, Thorley Lane, Manchester Airport, T0161-499 0500, www.etrophotel.co.uk. A beautiful Georgian country house hotel with an award-winning restaurant and 4-poster beds as well as lovely grounds. Great if you're coming from the airport and looking for somewhere. Some distance from the centre though.

££ Brooklands Lodge, 208 Marsland Rd, Sale, T0161-973 3283, www.brooklandslodge.co.uk. Charming B&B close to Brooklands metro. Rooms are en suite with flatscreen TV. Friendly and welcoming,

Apartments

There are a number of self-catering serviced apartments for short term rent. In the central area try **Lushpads**, www.lushpads.com; **Blue Rainbow Apartments**, www.bluerainbow apartments.com; **Light Boutique Aparthotel**, www.thelight.co.uk; **Dreamhouse Apartments**, www.dreamhouse apartments.com; **Roomzzz aparthotel**, www.roomzzz.co.uk; or **City Warehouse**, www.citywarehouseapartments.com.

Manchester *p18, map p22*

You won't go hungry in Manchester, a place with all the culinary variety you'd expect of a multicultural modern city. Chinatown and Rusholme have excellent Chinese and Indian restaurants respectively, and you can find some top modern English restaurants in the centre of town around King St. Budget student grub is served up in the Northern Quarter and around Oxford Rd, and if you're looking for a drink, they're also the places to check out. There's just about a pub on every corner, if not a trendy new wine bar.

£££ 39 Steps, 39 South King St, Deansgate, T0161-833 2432, www.39stepsrestaurant.co.uk. Serving gourmet fish in the city's finest and most recommended seafood restaurant, this is a classy, upmarket place to eat. Book ahead.

£££ The French at The Midland, Midland Hotel, Peter St, T0871-230 5347. Recently refurbished, the hotel restaurant has an impressive Edwardian interior. It's the most exclusive French restaurant in Manchester, but it can be booked up weeks in advance.

£££ Michael Caines @ ABode, 107 Piccadilly, T0161-247 7744, www.abode hotels.co.uk/manchester. Opened in 2007, this has become one of Manchester's top restaurants. A lively modern space with sophisticated ambience. The focus is on contemporary British food as well as tapas-style dishes, a tasting menu and cocktails.

£££-££ Australasia, 1 The Avenue, Spinningfields, T0161-831 0288, www.australasia.uk.com. Upmarket modern Australian cooking with Pacific Rim flavours. Turns into a lively bar after 2300.

£££-££ Livebait, 22 Lloyd St, T0161-817 4110, www.livebaitmanchester.com. Another of the city's snazzy fish restaurants, serving shellfish, including whelks, as well as tuna and swordfish. It's certainly not jellied eels, and the place has got a young professional buzz.

£££-££ River Bar and Restaurant, Lowry Hotel, 50 Dearmans Pl, T0161-827 4041, www.theriverrestaurant.com. Classy modern, restaurant overlooking the river, with modern and classic British dishes and an extensive wine list.

£££-££ Yang Sing, 34 Princess St, Chinatown, T0161-236 2200, www.yang-sing.com. Looks like nothing from the outside, but it receives consistently rave reviews and offers a superb range of delicacies and dim-sum. The lunchtime specials are good value.

££ Chaophraya, 19 Chapel Walks, T0161-832 8342, http://chaophraya.co.uk. Authentic Thai restaurant with good-value set menus or tempting à la carte specials such as scallops and black pudding or four seasons duck curry.

££ Koreana Restaurant, 40A King St West, T0161-832 4330, www.koreana.co.uk. One of the leading Asian restaurants outside Chinatown. The Korean barbecue is a particular speciality.

££ Northern Quarter, 108 High St, T0161-832 7115, www.tnq.co.uk. Friendly modern eatery with floor-to-ceiling windows. Classic dishes and a seasonal menu, all beautifully presented. Popular monthly themed evenings, as well as a 3-course 'Love Lunch'.

££ Rosso, King St, T0161-832 1400, www.rossorestaurants.com. Italian restaurant owned by Manchester United's Rio Ferdinand. Grade II listed building with original features including 2 restored domes, stained glass, marble columns and an ornate ceiling. The menu features well-made Italian classics.

££-£ Market Restaurant, 104 High St, T0161-834 3743, www.market-restaurant.com. Cosy family-run restaurant in the Northern Quarter specializing in English food, especially puddings. Freshly made food at decent prices.

£ Dimitri's, Campfield Arcade by Deansgate station, T0161-839 3319, www.dimitris.co.uk. With a small Mediterranean-based menu, **Dimitri's** has long been a favourite with locals, especially on a Fri and Sat evening when it serves up jazz along with the *dolmades*. Book in advance for weekends.

£ Grinch, 5-7 Chapel Walks, just off Cross St, T0161-907 3210, www.grinch.co.uk. A friendly, intimate and very good-value wine bar and restaurant with twisted metal light fittings and particularly good Italian and European food. It's got an even cheaper pre-theatre menu.

£ Soup Kitchen, 31-33 Spear St, T0161-236 5100, http://soup-kitchen.co.uk. Bustling community café in the Northern Quarter. As well as food and drink, it has live DJs, bands and events.

Cafés

Atlas, 376 Deansgate, T0161-834 2124, by Deansgate station, overlooking the canal, www.atlasbarmanchester.com. The delicious wholesome home-made food is served until 1430 daily and then it turns into a clubby bar later, open till 0200. Most of the other bars around Deansgate Station serve café-style lunches.

Earth Café, 16-20 Turner St, T0161-834 1996, www.earthcafe.co.uk. A good veggie place with changing daily menus and a juice bar. Great value organic food.

On The Eighth Day, 111 Oxford Rd, T0161-273 1850, http://eighth-day.co.uk. A vegetarian co-operative café and store that has been running since the 1970s. It's an authentic hippy hang-out complete with Buddhist chants soundtrack.

Teacup Café, 5 Thomas St, T0161-832 3233, http://teacupandcakes.com. From humble tea and cake to all-day breakfasts and filling mains such as cheeky moo pie or northern fettle samosa.

Manchester suburbs

£££ Aumbrey, 2 Church Lane, Prestwich, T0161-798 5841, www.aumbryrestaurant. co.uk. One of the best places to eat in the city. Chef Mary-Ellen McTague delivers beautiful

and delicious plates of food such as sautéed snails or pheasant pie. Great wine list too.

£££-££ Isinglass English Dining Room, 46 Flixton Rd, Urmston, T0161-749 8400, http://isinglassrestaurant.tumblr.com. Away from the centre but well worth the trip. The restaurant has a relaxed contemporary feel and the food is top-notch British, using only local ingredients.

£££-££ Lime Tree, 8 Lapwing Lane, West Didsbury, T0161-445 1217, www.thelimetree restaurant.co.uk. Elegant dining in a bohemian atmosphere, with a quality seasonal menu of British cuisine sourced from the owner's smallholding.

££ The Mark Addy, Stanley St, Salford, T0161-832 4080, www.markaddy.co.uk. Much more than a riverside pub, it serves up British classics alongside real ales. Fine dining in a great location.

Manchester *p18, map p22*
Manchester really comes alive after dark with clubs and bars of every description. The city is a lively place to be thanks to its huge student population, coupled with the distinct musical heritage of the place that brought you the likes of New Order, the Happy Mondays, Oasis and Badly Drawn Boy. The train service between Piccadilly and Oxford Rd and Deansgate means that it's easy to bar and club hop.

In general, bars in Manchester are open until around 0200 at the weekends and 1100-1200 during the week, longer if they are hosting events. **Canal St**, a short street packed with fashionable clubs and bars spilling out on to the streets, is well known for being one of the top gay attractions of England. This popularity gives it more of a mixed atmosphere at the weekend, but not during the week. **Oldham St** is one of the best places to sip a foreign beer in a trendy bar. **Deansgate Locks** is the place to go if your idea of a good night is dressing to the nines and sipping killer cocktails in bar-clubs surrounded by designer-clad beauties. It's the newest area to go out in and attracts a fashion-conscious, celeb crowd. Just follow the music from the train station to find the bars tucked away under the railway arches.

Pubs and bars

Britons Protection, 50 Great Bridgewater St, T0161-236 5895, www.britonsprotection.co.uk. Traditional English pub with a maze of rooms, lively atmosphere and large selection of whiskey. Decent good-value food.

Cloud 23, Beetham Tower, 303 Deansgate, T0161-870 1600, www.cloud23bar.com. Located in Manchester's highest building, this bar has floor-to-ceiling glass windows and the best view in town. With signature cocktails and an exclusive feel. Book in advance to avoid disappointment.

Cornerhouse Bar, 70 Oxford St, T0161-228 7621, www.cornerhouse.org. Opposite you as you walk out of the station. Shiny chrome surfaces and continental beers, attracting an older, more cultured clientele than some of the other bars.

Dry Bar, 28-30 Oldham St, T0161-236 9840, Dry Bar. Created in the early 1990s, then owned by Factory Records and New Order. They went bust and you're not likely to see Shaun Ryder propping up the bar these days, but it's still fairly hip and has a club atmosphere at the weekends.

Dukes 92, 18 Castle St, T0161-839 3522, www.dukes92.com. Originally a stable block, this waterside conversion has a spacious contemporary interior, with antique furniture such as chaise longues and deep armchairs. Limited but good bar and grill menu. There's a big outdoor terrace looking over the river.

Font Bar, 7-9 New Wakefield St, T0161-236 0944, http://thefontbar.wordpress.com/manchester. Famous for its cheap cocktails (£2-4) and continental beer selection, there's a quirky bohemian ambience with local artwork, vintage lamps and even a Playstation.

The Lass O'Gowrie, 36 Charles St, T0161-273 6932, www.thelass.co.uk. A more traditional pub popular with students.

The Marble Arch, 73 Rochdale Rd, T0161-832 5914, www.marblebeers.com. Cheery town pub with a Victorian interior, selection of locally brewed real ales and a beer garden.

Night and Day Café, 26 Oldham St, T0161-236 4597, www.nightnday.org. A daytime café serving Mexican dishes and a night-time bar. A laid-back vibe – more designer jeans and trainers than high heels and fake tan. The Twisted Nerve label, home of Badly Drawn Boy, hold a regular night here.

Odd Bar, 30-32 Thomas St, T0871-230 2208, www.oddbar.co.uk. Something of a Northern Quarter institution with a cosy atmosphere, free jukebox and monthly art exhibitions.

Odder Bar, 14 Oxford Rd, T0871-230 3662, http://odderbar.co.uk. **Odd's** sister bar. If you like giant lizards, huge vases and mirror-covered stairways, this is the place for you. This 2-storey bar with unconventional decor has a chilled-out vibe downstairs and live music and cool DJ nights upstairs in the newly opened **Function Room** club.

Revolution, 90-94 Oxford St, T0161-236 7470, www.revolution-bars.co.uk. The original Revolution bar, now a chain with others all across the country. The music is loud and clubby, attracting professionals and students. There's another branch at Deansgate Locks, Whitworth St West, T0161-839 7558, which is a little less scruffy than the Oxford Rd venue, again with bottled beers and vodka shots with sherbet dip and refresher flavours. Also at St Mary's Gate, Parsonage Gardens, T0161-839 9675,

Tribeca B.E.D Bar, 50 Sackville St, T0871-230 4455, www.tribeca-bar.co.uk. New York-style bar with a cosy mezzanine, large bar and sofa area. It's also the only bar in town with actual beds downstairs for you to lounge on. Low-key jazz in the background during by day, upbeat mainstream by night.

Soundtrack to the city

In the late 1980s, Factory Records and New Order decided that there were no clubs in Manchester that catered for their tastes. So they came up with one of their own. The Hacienda was a popular haunt with the musical sense to book Madonna for her first UK appearance. An explosion of local talent followed, and with the crossover of the dance music and indie music scenes, 'Madchester' took off. People all over the country started laying claim to Mancunian blood, and the university was massively oversubscribed with students wanting to spend their three years partying. You could spot Mancunian music a mile off, with the swirling Hammond organ of the Inspiral Carpets right through to the swagger of the Stone Roses and the Happy Mondays who dominated the charts. The scene, like The Hacienda, boomed and then bust, but not without laying the foundations of the new local and national independent music scene, which continues to thrive today.

Trof, The Deaf Institute, 135 Grosvenor St, www.trof.co.uk, T0161-276 9350. With a basement bar, ground floor café-bar and upstairs music hall hosting live music, open mic, 'hip hop karaoke' nights as well as regular club nights. There's a huge mirror ball, velvet curtains, domed ceiling and parrots on the wall. All good fun.

Via Manchester, 28-30 Canal St, T0161-236 6523, www.viamanchester.co.uk. Popular gay haunt. Free to get in.

Clubs

Many of the bars mentioned above have music and dancing. Manchester hasn't got all that many warehouse-sized venues but is peppered with smaller bars and intimate clubs which all have different characters and various types of music depending on the night. **Oxford Rd** is the place to come for Northern Soul and indie music as you'd expect from the nearby student population. **Deansgate Locks** is a little more dressy than some and most of the bars mentioned previously have dancing later on.

Attic, above The Thirsty Scholar, 50 New Wakefield St beside Oxford Rd station, T0161-236 6071, www.theatticmcr.co.uk. The best Northern Soul venue in town Thu-Sat. You'll not be allowed in a baseball cap or football shirt, but other than that it's pretty relaxed.

The Band on the Wall, 25 Swan St, T0161-834 1786, http://bandonthewall.org. Non-profit club run by the charity Inner City Music. Showcases live world music acts and have various clubby nights. DJ Mr Scruff has a monthly residency here.

Citrus, 2 Mount St, near the Town Hall, T0161-834 1344, www.citruslounge.co.uk. Open until 0100 and plays funky house. You have to pay an entry fee after 2400 but it's essentially a late bar with a small dance floor.

Contact Theatre, just after the Academy on Oxford Rd, T0161-274 0600, http://contact mcr.com. Hosts club nights on Fri and Sat and a few gay nights which are similarly cool.

Factory251, 112-118 Princess St, T0161-272 7251, www.factorymanchester.com. Set in the old headquarters of Manchester's Factory Records. 3 floors of different music, from indie, rock, reggae and pure cheese. Always popular so expect to queue to get in.

Jabez Clegg, 2 Portsmouth St, just off Oxford Rd, T0161-272 8612, www.jabezclegg.co.uk. Plays house and chart music in a dressed-down environment and is really popular.

The Manchester Academy, Oxford Rd, T0161-275 4278, www.manchester academy.net. Hosts indie nights during the week and is right next door to the Student Union. Trainers essential.

Po Na Na Souk Bar, 42 Charles St off Oxford Rd, T0161-272 6044, www.po nana.com. World music, jazz, hip-hop and all sorts in what feels like a dimly lit romantic boudoir.

Sankey's Soap, Beehive Mill, Radium St, T0161-236 5444, www.sankeys.info. Set in an old mill, it's head and shoulders above the rest for house and dance music. It's a place for high heels and short skirts rather than the scruffy student look, so make an effort and don't wear sportswear or you won't be allowed in. They have various touring top named DJs on a regular basis.

The Warehouse Project, Victoria Warehouse, Trafford Wharf Rd, T0161-835 3500, www.thewarehouseproject.com. A series of banging club nights that run Sep-Dec plus occasional weekend specials. The latest venue is a multi-room warehouse near Trafford Park with a spectacular line-up of electronic music nights that will blow your socks off. Has played host to DJs such as Sven Väth, Aphex Twin, Pete Tong and Erick Morillo, and musicians such as De La Soul, Happy Mondays, Jamiroquai and Dizzee Rascal. One of the best clubs in the country; tickets sell out fast.

⊙ Entertainment

Manchester *p18, map p22*
There's all sorts to keep you amused in Manchester, from massive multiplexes to small theatre companies and West End shows. Listings here are for venues in the centre of the city.

Theatre

Contact Theatre, just after the Academy on Oxford Rd, T0161-274 0600, http://contactmcr.com. This state-of-the-art theatre shows contemporary and innovative productions. It's a short bus ride from Oxford Rd on bus numbers 40-9 and also hosts R'n'B, gay and hip-hop club nights.

Library Theatre, currently showing work at The Lowry (see below), T0161-200 1536, www.librarytheatre.com. An intimate and classy theatre showing small productions for the more literary minded. Recently merged with Cornerhouse and will move to a new purpose-built venue on First St in 2014.

The Lowry, Pier 8, Salford Quays, T0843-208 6000, www.thelowry.com. Houses both the **Lyric** and the **Quays** theatres, showing touring productions and small plays from Zulu dancers to Shakespeare.

Opera House, 3 Quay St, T0870-060 1826, www.atgtickets.com/venues/opera-house-manchester. Shows mainly touring dramas and West End musicals.

Palace Theatre, Oxford St, T0161-245 6600, www.atgtickets.com/venues/palace-theatre-manchester. Does the same drama and musicals with the addition of some ballet and opera.

Royal Exchange, St Ann's Square, T0161-833 9833, www.royalexchange.co.uk. Described by Tom Courtenay as "a smaller world inside a greater one", the intimate theatre puts on superb productions from Oscar Wilde to Shakespeare and is highly recommended. They also have a bookshop, craft shops and a café and restaurant inside the complex. Beg, borrow or steal a ticket for a show here – they're worth it.

Cinema

Cornerhouse, 70 Oxford St, T0161-228 7621, www.cornerhouse.org. Opposite you as you walk out of the station. Has 3 screens that show the best of foreign and independent films.

Comedy
Comedy Store, Arches 3 and 4, Deansgate Locks, opposite Deansgate Station, T0161-839 9595, www.thecomedystore.co.uk. Attracts big names; check the website or *CityLife* to see what's on.
Frog and Bucket, 102 Oldham St, T0161-236 9805, www.frogandbucket.com. Award-winning comedy venue attracting some well-known comedians.

Live music
Music of every description from unsigned, unwashed indie bands to operatic divas can be found in Manchester. There are immense stadium gigs at the MEN arena right through to chamber music at the RNCM by talented classical performers.
Bridgewater Hall, Lower Mosely St, near the GMEX tram stop, T0161-950 9000, www.bridgewater-hall.co.uk. Housed in an impressive glass building, this is the home of Manchester Camerata and the Halle Orchestra. Expect nothing but the best in this venue with superb acoustics and a serene environment. Outside is a huge Japanese touchstone or *ishinki*. Stroking it means that you'll return one day. Guided tours take you backstage and around the building.
Manchester Academy, 296 Oxford Rd, T0161-275 2930, www.manchester academy.net. For rock, pop and indie.
Manchester Apollo, Stockport Rd, Ardwick Green, T08444-777677, www.o2apollo manchester.co.uk. Holding around 300 sweaty bodies for the latest rock and pop acts.
MEN Arena, T0161-950 5000, www.men-arena.com. A huge 1000-seater place for screaming teens coming to see the latest pop idol, and screaming mums coming to see the likes of Tom Jones on tour.
RNCM, 124 Oxford Rd, T0161-907 5200, www.rncm.ac.uk. Showcases a range of musical talent from brass bands to chamber music of the highest standard in an intimate atmosphere.

Manchester *p18, map p22*
Jan National Ales Festival, www.ale festival.org.uk/winterales. A celebration of more than 200 ales in **The Venue**.
May Future Everything. Experimental music and arts festival with local and international artists.
May-Sep Spinningfields, www.spinning fieldsonline.com. Outdoor cinema screens set up. Take a picnic and hire a deckchair.
Jun Manchester Day Parade www.themanchesterdayparade.co.uk. Street celebration of all things Mancunian.
Jul Manchester International Festival, www.mif.co.uk. Biennial festival showcasing original new work and special events.
Jul Manchester Jazz Festival, www.manchesterjazz.com. 2-week festival featuring jazz bands in outdoor and indoor venues.
Aug Manchester Pride, www.manchester pride.com. Manchester's gay pride festival, 10 days of floats, parades and partying.
Oct Manchester Comedy Festival, www.manchestercomedyfestival.com.
Oct Grim Up North, www.grimfest.com. A festival of all things spooky and gory.

Manchester *p18, map p22*
The Northern Quarter has an amazing array of boutiques and record shops. The **Craft and Design Centre**, 17 Oak St, www.craftand design.com, is a creative hub with artists studios and a shop for those one-off pieces.
Affleck's Palace, at the end of Tib St, T0161-834 2039, www.afflecks.com, has a labyrinthine 6 floors of clothes, knick-knacks, kitsch, fetish gear and fortune tellers. Across the road at 18 Oldham St is Manchester's best record shop, **Vinyl Exchange**, T0161-228 1122, www.vinylexchange.co.uk. It's heaven for music lovers looking to buy or sell

rarities, second-hand CDs or vinyl; anything goes really. Across the road are a number of dance music specialists. You'll certainly find what you're looking for, if not a local artist leafing through the record sleeves next to you. Also on Oldham St are a couple of vintage boutiques, such as **Retro Rehab**, 91 Oldham St, www.myspace.com/retro_rehab, and the **Pop Boutique**, 34-36 Oldham St, www.pop-boutique.com. For designer labels and more high-street shopping, **King Street** is upmarket with DKNY and Armani stores amongst others. **The Triangle** in the Millennium Quarter is a fashionable shopping centre designed just for these top-of-the range brands and is full of well-coiffeured and perfumed women.

▲ What to do

Manchester *p18, map p22*
Cricket
Lancashire County Cricket Club, Old Trafford, Old Trafford Metrolink, T0161-282 4000, www.lccc.co.uk. Tickets available for 1-day and Test matches during the season.

Football
There are 8 professional football teams in the Greater Manchester area, with the giants of Manchester City and Manchester United battling it out in the premier league. Tickets are hard to come by due to their popularity but both stadiums offer tours.
Manchester City, Etihad Stadium, Etihad Campus, T0161-4441894, www.mcfc.co.uk. The home of Manchester City since 2003. Adults £12, concessions £9.
Manchester United, North Stand, Old Trafford, Sir Matt Busby Way, T0161-868 8000 www.manutd.com. Museum and tour £16, concessions £10.50. See page 24 for details.
Stockport County, Edgerley Park near Stockport station, T08456-885799, www.stockportcounty.com. If you want to

see good northern football, have a meat pie and watch a game untainted by the big bucks, tickets are usually available up to kick-off, Sat afternoons and Tue evenings, £18 adult, £11 concession, £3 child (7-16).

⊖ Transport

Manchester *p18, map p22*
Bus
National Express, T08705-808080, runs 11 services a day from Chorlton St bus station to and from **London Victoria** (5 hrs). They go 12 times a day to **Birmingham** (3 hrs), 6 times to **Edinburgh** (7 hrs), 6 times to **Gatwick airport** (7 hrs via Birmingham and Heathrow) and 12 times to **Heathrow** (5½ hrs). Services to **Liverpool** are hourly (1 hr) and there are 7 daily services to **Stansted Airport** (6½ hrs). **Stagecoach**, T01772-884488, runs the X61 hourly to **Blackpool**, (1½ hrs) and there is a Transpeak, T01773-536336, service to **Nottingham** (3 hrs) through the **Peak District** via Buxton (1 hr), Matlock and Bakewell. **Eurolines**, T08705-143219, www.gobycoach.com, also run to major European cities via London

Car
Easycar, NCP car park, Chatham St, www.easycar.com, T09063-333333. **Hertz**, Auburn St across from Piccadilly Station, T08708-484848 (closed Sun), www.hertz.com. **Sixt Kenning**, Manchester Airport Terminals 1, 2 and 3, T0161-489 2666, www.e-sixt.co.uk.

Train
Virgin Trains are the main service to and from Manchester, T0870-010 1127, www.virgin trains.co.uk. They go hourly to **London Euston** from Manchester Piccadilly, Mon-Sat until 2000, taking 3 hrs. There are regular trains to **Birmingham** (1 hr) and **Liverpool** (1 hr). From Manchester Piccadilly you can also get to **Glasgow** in 4 hrs.

The Peak District

At the southern end of the Pennine Hills between Manchester and Sheffield sits the Peak District National Park, an oasis in the heart of the Northwest's built-up areas. In 1932 the ninth Duke of Devonshire, the biggest private landowner in the Peak District, set his gamekeepers on trespassers who had ventured onto his grouse moors on Kinder Scout. Five of them were subsequently jailed for up to six months, but it was this trespass and the resulting furore that brought about the existence of this and Britain's 10 other national parks. Nowadays, of course, you're free to roam over the 555 square miles of moorland, dales, rocky cliffs and skyline-shattering tors which lie across six counties. Its proximity to the metropolitan areas of the Midlands and the Northwest, as well as its beauty, have made the Peak District one of Britain's most visited national parks.

The spa town Buxton is a nexus in the area, the source of the natural mineral water which is still the lifeblood of the town. Presiding over the southeast of the Peak District, the immense pile of Chatsworth House, home of the Duke and Duchess of Devonshire, welcomes visitors and is surrounded by a number of characterful stone villages. The Peak District is primarily walking territory, though, and Dovedale, Edale and the High Peak are the places to exercise your legs, with views to delight all from the hardy hiker to the picnic-loving day tripper.

The Peak District

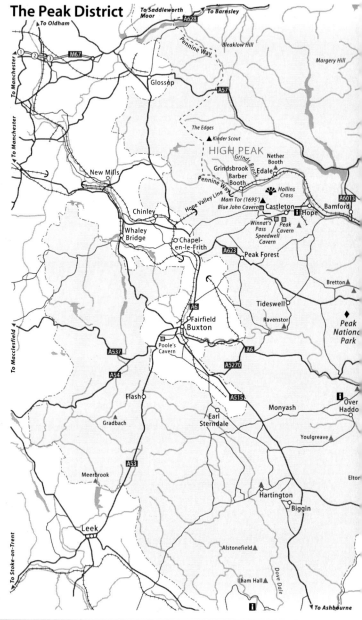

Arriving in the Peak District

Getting there Manchester Airport (see page 19), is the closest airport, about 25 miles away by road, and has daily flights from the UK and abroad. You can get to the Peak District from here on the regular train service changing at Manchester Piccadilly for Buxton.

Macclesfield is on the London Euston–Manchester intercity rail route, from where you can easily reach Buxton. Trains run several times a day. The Peak District is well-served by the Hope Valley train line (see Getting around, below), which is accessible from Chesterfield, Derby and Sheffield. Contact **National Rail Enquiries** ① *T08457-484950, www.nationalrail.co.uk*, for details, or www.thetrainline.com.

Situated between Manchester, Sheffield and Derby, the road access here is good. The Peak District is linked to Manchester and Derby by the A6, Chesterfield by the A619 and Sheffield by the A625. **National Express** ① *T08705-808080, www.nationalexpress. co.uk*, runs a coach service from London via Derby, Loughborough and Leicester into Buxton. ▸▸ *See Transport, page 53.*

Getting around The public transport network in the Peak District is not too bad at all, especially considering that all the locals have cars to get around in. The bus and train services are especially useful if you're doing a non-circular walk. If you're driving, be aware that the 500,000 drivers a year that this area attracts have an enormous environmental impact on the scenery. By train there's the **Hope Valley Line**, which runs from Manchester to Sheffield calling at New Mills, Chinley, Edale, Hope, Bamford, Hathersage, Grindleford and Dore. Trains run a couple of times an hour in both directions, with the last train at around 2200. From Manchester Piccadilly it takes just over an hour to get to Sheffield, and it takes

45 minutes to New Mills Central. From Buxton, you need to take a train to New Mills to join the Hope Valley Line, a service that runs at least three times an hour and takes 30 minutes. The **Derbyshire Wayfarer Ticket** allows a day's unlimited travel on buses and trains in Derbyshire, which you can buy at most TICs and bus travel offices for £11.10 adult (plus one child) and £5.55 concessions/child. It's a good idea if you want to cover a lot of ground quickly, and you can get from Buxton to Sheffield on this service easily, taking in all the little villages in between. Contact **Traveline** ① *T0870-6082608, http://traveline.info*, for details.

Orientation The major walking area in the Peak District is in the centre around Edale. Dovedale in the south is also very popular, and there are pleasant short walks to be had all over the national park as you'd expect. Small stone villages are dotted all over the place, with the most interesting being Castleton, complete with labyrinthine caves through the limestone hills and Eyam, a village struck by the Black Death in the 17th century which has avoided tourist trappings that plague other villages. The southeast of the park has the small market towns of Matlock and Bakewell, and the only place not really worth checking out is the northern area of Saddleworth Moor, unless you're a big fan of bleak, misty barren areas. It's the exception in an otherwise geologically interesting area with wide variety in its peaks, plains and sunny dales. For maps try: Ordnance Survey *Buxton and Matlock OS Landranger 119*; *Sheffield and Huddersfield OS Landranger 110*; *The White Peak OL 24*; and *The Dark Peak Explorer OL1*.

Geology
Wind-blown boggy moors, hay meadows, sunny dales and rocky outcrops shouldn't really exist together, but they do. This contrast in landscape is all down to the interactions between two types of rock in the Peak District: **Millstone Grit** and **Limestone**.

The White Peak is a limestone plateau of gentle rolling dales split with river valleys. The softer landscape is underpinned with the porous limestone rock, easily dissolved by the slightly acidic rain into great caverns underground. The subterranean passages in this area are thick with cavers, squeezing themselves through the skinny tunnels in search of cathedral-like areas of grand and weird natural phenomena.

High above these mad pot-holers, the climbers of the Peak District make use of the other geological feature, the **Millstone Grit**. This stone is very hard-wearing, and you can see examples of the old millstones scattered over **the Dark Peak**. It's also used in many of the churches of the northwest area, a not very pretty dark and dirty stone, but one which wears well against the elements. This hard cliff creates the rocky outcrops and splintered faces of the more dramatic tors in the national park, the Edges, which are unique in the British landscape. Climbers cling to the crags here. The aspect of Kinder Scout is the most impressive view of Millstone Grit that you'll see in the Peaks.

The conjunction of these two, the rough with the smooth, makes for very interesting scenery whose variety will surely keep everyone happy in one way or another.

Buxton → *For listings, see pages 49-53.*

Enclosed by the national park to the south, east and west, Buxton is a small Victorian town central to the district although not strictly part of it. The Romans discovered the mineral springs here in AD 78 that are still regarded as Buxton's lifeblood today in the form of Buxton Mineral Water. It became a fashionable spa resort in the early 19th century when the Duke of Devonshire improved the hotels, walks and baths. The Georgian-style Crescent was built in imitation of Bath, and the town is not unlike Bath in its feel – but without the hordes of tourists and, unfortunately, without any surviving baths to look round. Buxton really comes alive in the summer with the **Buxton Festival**, which draws artists and enthusiasts from miles around for an excellent week of musical enjoyment.

Arriving in Buxton
Getting there and around Regular intercity trains run from London Euston to Manchester, and there are connecting services to Buxton from Macclesfield and Stockport en route, which take roughly 30 minutes. Buxton is only an hour's drive from Manchester, Derby, Nottingham and Sheffield. **National Express** ① *www.nationalexpress.co.uk*, has a daily coach service to Buxton from London via Derby, Leicester and Loughborough. The local bus network runs through the Peak District via Buxton between Manchester, Derby and Nottingham and from Sheffield, Stoke-on-Trent, Ashbourne and Macclesfield.

Buxton

Where to stay 🛏		Old Hall **9**
Buckingham **5**		
Buxton Hostel **3**		**Restaurants** 🍴
Grendon Guest House **6**		Columbine **1**
Grin Low Campsite **8**		Old Clubhouse **2**
Limetree Park Campsite **2**		Wild Carrot **3**
Lowther Guest House **7**		

100 metres
100 yards

Tourist information Buxton TIC ⓘ *Pavilion Gardens, St Johns Rd, T01298-25106, www.visitpeakdistrict.com, www.visitbuxton.co.uk, daily 0900-1700*, is the main TIC for the Peak District and can book accommodation. The centre contains informative displays and exhibitions by local artists and craftsmen. Pick up a copy of the magazine *Pure*, www.purebuxton.co.uk, for details of local events and listings.

Places in Buxton

The Crescent, undeniably Buxton's most dominant architectural presence, was built in 1780-1784 and intended to rival the famous Royal Crescent in Bath. It's now a listed building undergoing massive refurbishment by English Heritage. Directly opposite is a small fountain, **St Anne's Well**, a public pump built by the eighth Duke of Devonshire to let the people of Buxton have a free supply of their famous water. It comes out of the pump at 28°C and usually has a stream of locals standing beside it filling containers. Next to that is the **Pump Room** where once visitors took the thermal waters; it is now used to display the work of local artists. Behind that you've got **The Slopes**, public gardens on a bit of a hill with a view of the cobblestone town from one side and the shadow of the Peaks on the other.

On The Square is the **Old Hall**, Buxton's oldest building dating from 1573 and now a hotel. Mary Queen of Scots stayed here when she visited the town to take the waters in a bid to alleviate her rheumatism. Walking past this, you come to **Buxton Opera House**, the town's main attraction, designed by Frank Matcham in 1903. It's immensely popular in the summer when it holds the spectacular **Buxton Opera Festival** and also the **International Gilbert and Sullivan Festival**, both of which bring the town alive (see Festivals, page 53). The **Pavilion Gardens** beside it are classic Victorian landscaping.

If it's raining, or even if it isn't, the **Museum and Art Gallery** ⓘ *Terrace Rd, T01298-533540, Tue-Fri 0930-1730, Sat 0930-1700, Sun 1030-1700*, is well worth a visit. Downstairs there's an exhibition tracing the contemporary multiculturalism of the region through individuals' life stories, from miners to farmers and refugees, and upstairs is an award-winning history of human life in the Peak District from the Stone Age to the present day.

Poole's Cavern

ⓘ *Green Lane, T01298-26978, www.poolescavern.co.uk. Daily 0930-1700. £8.80, £7.80 concessions, child £5. Tours run every 20 mins; it can be chilly inside so don't forget a jumper.*
Just under a mile from Buxton is Poole's Cavern, below the limestone landscape of Grinlow Hill in Buxton Country Park. It contains the biggest stalactite and stalagmite in the Peak District and a load of weird and wonderful formations. The cavern is named after a medieval highwayman who hid in it and apparently buried both his treasure and his victims here. If you visit at the time of the Buxton Festival you'll be treated to a tour by candlelight, which is quite spectacular. The atmospheric tour takes 45 minutes.

The murder at Winnat's Pass

In the 18th-century, the nearby town of Peak Forest had the status of a southern Gretna Green, where couples could marry without living in the parish. In the mid-1770s, a young and affluent couple, Alan and Clara, decided to elope there. Stopping in Castleton on the way to Peak Forest, they rested in one of the village's many coaching inns, their wealth and status as out-of-towners clear to all present. Their conversation was overheard by six miners at a nearby table. The next day their bodies were discovered scattered across Winnat's Pass, robbed of all possessions. The miners were suspected of their murder, but no conclusive proof was ever found. In a spooky turn of events, each of the six miners was found dead in unpleasant or unexplained circumstances during the following year.

The Hope Valley → *For listings, see pages 49-53.*

Driving north on the A6 from Buxton to Chapel-en-le-Frith and then taking the A623 and B6049 out of town, you'll come to the Hope Valley. It's real Goretex and gaiters country, with its epicentre at Edale, the start of the Pennine Way. Mam Tor nearby towers over the pretty village of Castleton with its Norman castle and subterranean cave network. It's not just a walking area here, though; there's all manner of other activities from caving to hang-gliding and probably the odd management group out on team-building exercises. A little further on is the small village of Eyam, whose fame as the plague village of the 17th century that submitted itself to voluntary quarantine to stop the spread of disease, is out of all proportion to its size.

Castleton

This beautiful, if touristy, village in the heart of the Peak District boasts underground caves, a Norman castle and a dramatic approach through Winnat's Pass, a steep descent of 1300 ft. The pass is rocky, treacherous and has a heart-stopping view. To put it in context, if you were to ride down it on a bike, you'd be in Sheffield before you had to start pedalling. The area was heavily mined for lead and the mineral **Blue John**, found nowhere else in the world, and the resulting caves and caverns are now top tourist attractions, taking you deep into the middle of the earth, while the stone twinkles in the window of every single tourist shop in the village. The area is a great base for walking and outdoor activities too, and the caverns are worth visiting if you need to shelter from the rain.

Arriving in Castleton The Manchester–Sheffield train stops at Hope and Edale where linking buses take you into Castleton. Information is available from the small **Castleton Visitor Centre** ① *Buxton Rd, at the entrance to the main village car park, T01433-620679, www.visitpeakdistrict.com, daily 1000-1700 with seasonal variations.*

Places in Castleton Put the brakes on as you come to the bottom of Winnat's Pass and you'll find the best of the four underground caves in Castleton. The **Speedwell Cavern** ① *T01433-620512, www.speedwellcavern.co.uk, Apr-Oct daily 1000-1700, Nov-Mar daily 1000-1600, £9.25, concessions £8.25, child £7.25; discounts if also visiting Peak Cavern (below); take a jumper, it's cold and damp down there,* takes you down through an airlock and on to a boat to explore the underground world. The guides are fun and informative, and you can see claustrophobic tunnels carved out by the miners as well as the natural caves and stalactites and stalagmites.

Further into the village you'll find the **Peak Cavern** ① *T01433-620285, www.peak cavern.co.uk, Apr-Oct daily 1000-1700, Nov-Mar weekends only 1000-1700, £8.75, concessions £7.75, child £6.75, 2 tours per day at 1100 and 1400,* trumpeting about its alternative name, 'The Devil's Arse', where you walk into the limestone gorge below Peveril Castle on an hour-long tour.

There's more of the same, without the attention-seeking name, at **Treak Cliff Cavern** ① *T01433-620571, www.bluejohnstone.com, Mar-Oct 1000-1700 last tour 1615, Nov-Feb 1000-1600 last tour 1515, £8.75, concessions £7.75, child £4.75.* And also **Blue John Cavern** ① *T01433-620638, www.bluejohn-cavern.co.uk, £9, concessions £7, child £4.50,* which has a 45-minute tour of the caves.

Overlooking Castleton is all 1695 ft of **Mam Tor**. Meaning 'mother mountain', it's known locally as the 'shivering mountain' because it is composed of crumbling layers of gritstone and shale which produce frequent, small landslips. It's an easy walk up because it has a stepped footpath, ideal if you're not a true walker. The views from the top show the limestone quarries, not too pretty, but try and imagine it 5000 years ago when it was a Bronze Age fort. You'll also see flocks of hang-gliders taking off and enjoying the scenery.

Peveril Castle ① *(EH), Market Place, T01433-620613, Apr-Oct daily 1000-1800, Nov-Mar weekends only 1000-1600, £4.50, concessions £4.10, child £2.70,* overlooks Castleton. A Norman Castle given by William the Conqueror to William Peverel, his illegitimate son, it has a fantastic view and is a lovely spot for a picnic but unfortunately you have to pay to walk round it as it's owned by English Heritage. There's nothing to see but spacious views and the ruins.

Edale

A pleasant walk from the centre of Castleton to Hollin's Cross will take you to Edale. It's also reachable by train on the Hope Valley line from Hope station and, as the beginning of the **Pennine Way**, is undoubtedly the most popular place to walk in the Peaks. The Way stretches from here through the High Peak, into the Yorkshire Dales and the Cheviot Hills and ends right up in the Scottish Borders. Opened in 1965 as the UK's first long-distance path, it's a walk of 289 miles (463 km) up the backbone of England from Edale to Kirk Yetholm in Scotland. It takes at least two weeks of solid walking across moorland and is a truly rewarding hike, but you need to be prepared for it. The high rainfall in the upland area and the possibility of heatwaves make it unpredictable as far as the weather is concerned, and you need to know how to use a map and compass. The best time of year to go is in the summer between late May and September. A number of walkers' books are available about the route, including Wainwright's *Pennine Way Companion*.

A nice afternoon's walk can be had up the glacial valley to the top of the dominant plateau of **Kinder Scout**. It takes about two hours to reach the commanding views at the

"Greater love hath no man than this: that he lay down his life for his fellow man"

In September 1665, a small box of cloth was delivered from London to a tailor's assistant George Viccars in Eyam. The material was damp when he got it so he spread it out to dry. Within days Viccars fell ill and died, becoming the first of Eyam's victims of the Bubonic Plague.

In the following months, the plague took hold in the village and those who could fled to the moorland around in desperation to escape. Anxious to avoid further contagion, Eyam's rector William Mompesson consulted the villagers and asked them to quarantine themselves. The villagers agreed. Mompesson arranged with the Earl of Devonshire at Chatsworth House that food and medication should be left at two points on the edge of the village, the boundary stone to the south and what is now called Mompesson's well to the north. To pay for these items the villagers left money in the holes drilled into the stone, which were filled with vinegar to prevent infection. Thinking that the plague was an airborne infection – actually carried by fleas, so they weren't too far off – church services were suspended and open-air sermons were conducted in Cucklett Delph, a valley nearby. There were also no public funerals for the same reason, and families buried their own. One lady, Mrs Hancock of Riley was in the sad situation of having to bury her husband and six children in an eight-day period.

In October 1666 the plague ended. A village that had previously numbered 350 in 76 families in 1665 was left with only 270 people. The selfless act of the villagers is remembered each year on Plague Sunday, the last Sunday in August, with a service at Cucklett Delph.

top on the **Grindsbrook Path**, a well-worn walking trail that turns into the Pennine Way a little later. It is nose-to-tail most of the way here on a sunny Sunday as people from Sheffield and Manchester forsake the city for the dramatic scenery. It's a well-marked trail and you can't get lost: just take the path behind the **Old Nag's Head** pub and walk up alongside the river.

Eyam

Don't be surprised if you can't find anywhere to park in this small village or if you're assailed by hordes of schoolchildren waving clipboards at you on a weekday. Eyam (pronounced 'eem') is famous for being the plague village where from 1665 to 1666 the villagers underwent a voluntary quarantine to protect others from catching the Black Death (see box, above). Primary schoolchildren know the story better than anyone. It's a pretty place to explore, and there are lovely walks to be had in this area.

The best place to begin your exploration of Eyam is the **Eyam Museum** ① *Hawkhill Rd, T01433-631371, www.eyammuseum.demon.co.uk, Mar-Nov Tue-Sun 1000-1630, closed Mon except bank holidays, £2.50, £2 concessions/child*, at the top of the village. It explores the early history of plague in the village in detail with a strong anecdotal focus on how it affected individuals. Downstairs is a smaller display about the silk and cotton industries which, alongside mining and quarrying, make up the village's more recent history.

From the museum you can walk into town where you'll find the **Plague cottages**: pretty, residential stone cottages with plaques on the outside walls showing gruesome death tallies. The medieval **Eyam Parish Church** is also just off the main road and has a small exhibition inside about the plague. It has a far older history than this though, with a Saxon font and a Saxon cross in the graveyard outside. Don't be shy about looking round; it's all trampled by schoolchildren on a daily basis as they hurdle gravestones in search of plague victims. From the church there's a pleasant walk (1 km) across the fields to **Mompesson's Well** on the outskirts of the village.

Back in the centre of the village is the **Eyam Hall and Craft Centre** ① *T01433-631976, www.eyamhall.co.uk, Tue-Sun 1030-1700, Nov-Feb closes at 1600; house and gardens, Jun-Sep and school holidays Wed, Thu, Sun 1100-1600, £7.50, child £4.* The hall is a 17th-century farmhouse with lovely gardens and a less emotive history.

Bakewell → *For listings, see pages 49-53.*

The best thing about Bakewell, roughly five miles from Eyam, is also its major claim to fame – the delicious almond pastry cakes known as Bakewell puddings. These first came about when someone tried to bake a Christmas cake and got it all wrong. Originally an old Saxon market town, it's now a large village or small town, easily reached from Buxton or Chesterfield, with a small shopping centre, public gardens and a river running through it under a stone bridge. But the major sights in the area, Haddon Hall and Chatsworth House, just outside the town, are what often bring people here.

Tourist information
The **Bakewell Visitor Centre** ① *Old Market Hall, Bridge St, T01629-816558, www.peak district.org, Apr-Oct 0930-1730, Nov-Mar 1000-1700*, in the centre of town has information on accommodation. A useful website is www.bakewellonline.co.uk.

Around Bakewell
Two miles south of Bakewell on the A6, **Haddon Hall** ① *T01629-812855, www.haddon hall.co.uk; May-Sep daily 1200-1700 (last admission 1600), with late opening on Thu; Apr/Oct Sat-Mon 1030-1630, closed Nov-Feb; £10, concessions £9.50, child £5.50*, is a real delight in an idyllic setting. It's a beautiful medieval hall with Tudor additions set high on the hill with views of the surrounding area and a babbling offshoot of the River Wye passing under a stone bridge. Owned by the Manners family for 800 years, the walled gardens are very romantic, and inside the hall you can walk round the Tudor bedrooms and the medieval chapel with its original heraldic wall paintings pretending to be a lord or lady taking some exercise in the long gallery. It's a quintessentially English scene and totally unmissable on a lovely day. Compared with its neighbour, Chatsworth House, Haddon Hall is much more intimate and manageable in size.

Chatsworth House and Gardens ① *8 miles north of Bakewell, T01246-565300, www.chatsworth.org; house and garden, Mar-Dec daily 1100-1730, £19, £17 concessions, child £13; garden only, £10, concessions £8, child £6; farmyard and adventure playground, Mar-Dec daily, 1100-1730, £6; park open year round, free*, is a huge 16th-century country estate known as the Palace of the Peak. Allow plenty of time to explore this palatial residence, which could easily take all day, and wear some comfortable shoes. The

105-acre garden is 450 years old and contains a maze, cottage gardens, five miles of wooded walks with rare trees and shrubs and a 200 m cascading waterfall. There's also a brilliant adventure playground up amid the trees and a working farmyard for children. The Duke and Duchess of Devonshire still live at Chatsworth and are actively involved in its upkeep. The house has hundreds of richly decorated rooms, historic paintings and sculptures including works by Holbein, Rembrandt and Gainsborough. The Orangery in the gardens has some lovely craft shops and a café.

Matlock and Matlock Bath → *For listings, see pages 49-53.*

Matlock is one of the larger towns in the Peak District. Surrounded by hills and overlooked by a folly, Riber Castle, it's reasonably picturesque with a few good places to stay and eat but little in the way of tourist attractions; the real treasures lie outside the town. Matlock Bath, on the other hand, a couple of miles down the road, has plenty of child-friendly attractions: a cable car to a cave-riddled tourist centre, a Gulliver's Kingdom and an aquarium. Although its setting is undoubtedly striking, in a gorge with the River Derwent running through, these days it is awash with chip shops, amusement arcades and tacky trinket shops. In summer it becomes a haven for motorbikers attracted by the challenging, sweeping Derbyshire roads.

Arriving in Matlock and Matlock Bath
Getting there Regular train services go to Matlock and Matlock Bath from Derby. The Transpeak bus service runs every two hours between Nottingham and Manchester, calling at Derby, Belper, Matlock, Bakewell, Buxton and Manchester. For travel information contact **Traveline** ⓘ *T0871-200 2233, http://traveline.info.* **National Express** ⓘ *T08717-818178, www.nationalexpress.co.uk,* also runs a daily coach service to Matlock from London Victoria. By car, Matlock is 25 miles north of Derby on the A6, 10 miles southwest of Chesterfield on the A632 and eight miles west of Alfreton on the A632.

Tourist information Matlock Visitor Information Point ⓘ *Peak Rail Shop, Matlock Station, T01335-343666, www.derbyshiredales.gov.uk, daily 1000-1700,* and also at **Matlock Bath** ⓘ *The Pavilion, South Parade, T01629-583834, Apr-Oct daily 1000-1700, Nov-Mar Wed-Fri 1100-1500, Sat-Sun 1100-1600.* The website www.matlock.org.uk also provides useful information about the area.

Places in Matlock and Matlock Bath
The Edwardian spa town became less popular towards the end of the 19th century, and there's not much left to see of the actual spa today. On a rainy day, you could visit the **Aquarium** ⓘ *110 North Parade, T01629-583624, www.matlockbathaquarium.co.uk, Easter-Oct 1000-1730, Nov-Apr weekends 1000-1700, £2.90, children under 4 free,* found in the old Matlock Bath Hydro, complete with marble staircase and thermal pool which now comforts the aches and pains of koi carp rather than the ladies and gents of the town.

Also in Matlocok Bath is the **Peak Mining Museum and Temple Mine** ⓘ *The Pavilion, T01629-583834, www.peakmines.co.uk; museum Easter-Oct daily 1000-1700, Nov-Apr Wed-Sun 1100-1500; temple mine Easter-Oct daily at 1200 and 1400, Nov-Apr weekends only at 1200 and 1400; museum or mine, £3.50, child £2.50; joint ticket £6, child £4,* with hands-on exhibits and a maze of twisting tunnels. It's a real insight into the industry which shaped so much of the area.

Riber Castle ⓘ *free*, at the top of the hill is a ruined 19th-century castle built and designed by local textile designer John Smedley who founded Matlock's hydros. It has been unoccupied for many years, hence its romantic and ruined appearance. Take a walk up the hill to see it for yourself.

A couple of miles to the south of Matlock Bath are **The Heights of Abraham** ⓘ *T01629-582365, www.heightsofabraham.com, Apr-Nov daily 1000-1630, limited opening in Feb-Mar, £13, £9.50 concessions, children £9*, where cable cars take you up above the Derwent River Valley to a limestone cliff. At the top you can go underground into the show caves and find out more about the mining history of the area. There's also an adventure playground for children, and the view is breathtaking. It's a fully organized and commercial take on the countryside that you can see just as well by going for a walk independently, although the cable cars are fun.

Walks around Matlock

The visitor centre has six free leaflets on walks around Matlock town, all of which take a couple of hours, are relatively easy-going and a highly recommended insight into the area and its heritage. They include the 3½-mile **Cuckoostone Walk**, a circular walk taking you from Chesterfield Road up to the Matlock moor area with views of Riber Castle, and the **Wellfield Walk**, which takes you up to Lumsdale, one of the oldest industrial valleys in England and the wishing stone. (If you walk round it three times and leave some money on it, your dreams *will* come true.) There are a number of other walks around the area, and the tourist office in Matlock provides comprehensive information on them, as does the YHA.

Nine Ladies ⓘ *3 miles northwest of Matlock, look for signs pointing to Stanton-in-Peak, Stanton Lees or Birchover*, on Stanton Moor is a Bronze Age stone circle enclosed by a small circular bank beside a wood, unfortunately under threat from quarrying in this area. The 3000- to 4000-year-old burial ground of Stanton Moor is dotted about with over 70 cairns and is an atmospheric and peaceful grove particularly first thing in the morning when there are fewer dog walkers around. Folklore has it that the circle is made of people who were turned to stone as punishment for dancing on the Sabbath, with the 'fiddler', a few yards away, turned into the King stone.

The Peak District listings

For hotel and restaurant price codes and other relevant information, see pages 9-12.

😊 Where to stay

Buxton *p41, map p41*

Buxton has some wonderful slabs of Victorian architecture, grand hotels that look like they'd be more at home in Brighton than the wilds of Derbyshire. There's also a number of homely B&Bs in stone cottages dotted about the town. Book all accommodation in advance in the summer – rooms fill up quickly during the opera season.

£££-££ Biggin Hall, Biggin-by-Hartington, 11 miles from Buxton, T01298-84451, www.bigginhall.co.uk. A fabulously romantic 17th-century pile which boasts air so pure that it supposedly soothes asthmatics and insomniacs. The bedrooms are stunning, huge low-beamed affairs with 4-poster beds and antiques, and there are log fires in the sitting rooms and a library. There's also traditional farmhouse cooking.

££ Barms Farm, a mile north of Buxton at Fairfield, T01298-77723, www.barmsfarm .co.uk. The pick of the B&Bs round here. The good-value but luxury rooms are light and airy in this non-smoking country farmhouse.

££ Buckingham Hotel, 1 Burlington Rd, T01298-70481, www.buckinghamhotel.co.uk. A small and leafy hotel with friendly 'free spirited' staff and a homely, laid-back atmosphere. It's fairly upmarket with a plush bar and dining room.

££ Fernydale Farm, just 5 miles from Buxton at Earl Sterndale, T01298-83236, www.fernydalefarmbandb.co.uk. Bed and hearty breakfasts are on offer at this pretty white-stone cottage on a small working farm. From Buxton, take the A515 to Ashbourne for about 3 miles and it is signposted from there.

££ Grendon Guest House, Bishops Lane off St John's Rd, T01298-78831, www.grendon guesthouse.co.uk. An Edwardian house with gardens and views across the hills. It's on a bit of a hill, like most of Buxton, and you'll be well looked after.

££ The Old Hall Hotel, The Square, T01298-22841, www.oldhallhotelbuxton.co.uk. Centrally located in Buxton itself, this is where Mary Queen of Scots is said to have stayed and is the oldest hotel in town. It's proud of its history and is a traditional old hotel offering bed and breakfast and rooms with 4-poster beds and wood-pannelled walls.

££-£ Lowther Guest House, 7 Hardwick Sq West, T01298-71479, www.lowtherguest house.co.uk. A little cheaper, this is a small and homely place. Easter-Oct. Credit cards not accepted.

£ Buxton Hostel, Sherbrook Lodge, Harper Hill Rd, T01298-25106, www.youth hostelsguide.com/hostels/view/32. It's in wooded grounds 1½ miles from the station. Open from 1700.

Camping

Grin Low, by Poole's Cavern, T01298-77735.
Limetree Park, T01298-22988, www.limetreeparkbuxton.com.

Castleton *p43*

Most places in Castleton itself are unpretentious, walker-friendly and reasonably priced.

£££ The Castle Hotel, Castle St, T01433-620578, www.vintageinn.co.uk/thecastlecastleton. Really an old pub in the centre of the village, this is the only luxury accommodation here, 6 of its rooms containing jacuzzis, perfect after a long walk, and 4-poster beds. It is 350 years old, has wholesome pub food and welcomes walkers.

££ Causeway House, T01433-623291, www.causewayhouse.co.uk. One of many stone cottage B&Bs on the road out from the village towards Hope.

£ Castleton Losehill Hall YHA, Hope Valley, T0845-3719628, www.yha.org.uk/hostel/castleton-losehill-hall. Newly refurbished Gothic mansion set in 27 acres of parkland with formal gardens, woods and streams. Close to Winnats Pass and Mam Tor. Ideal for activity-based holidays.

Camping
Losehill Caravan Club Site, Hope Valley, T01433-620636.

Edale *p44*
There are a number of stone cottages with the odd room let out as B&B accommodation in Edale. They're all walker-friendly and homely places to stay.
£££ Stonecroft, Grindsbrook, Edale, T01433-670262, www.stonecroftguesthouse.co.uk. Charming house with lovely views. Rooms are en suite or have private bathroom. Breakfast is served in the period dining room.
£££-££ Mam Tor House, Edale, T01433-670253, www.mamtorhouse.co.uk. Loft conversion in a converted wing of the main Edwardian house. Both rooms are en suite. Private gardens and parking.
££-£ Ollerbrook Barn, Ollerbrook Booth, T01433-670200, www.ollerbrook-barn-cottage.co.uk. B&B in a barn conversion ¼ mile from Edale with spectacular views.
£ Edale YHA, Rowland Cote, Nether Booth, on the wooded hillside of the Kinder plateau, T0845-371 9514, www.yha.org.uk/hostel/edale. Good for activities and activity groups. In the middle of a network of footpaths.

Camping
There are also numerous farms who will let you pitch your tent in a field for a small price. No mod cons here, but at least it's cheap.
Fieldhead Campsite, T01433-670386, www.fieldhead-campsite.co.uk. Lovely peaceful site, owned by the Peak District National Park Authority and located at the Visitor Information Centre.

Ollerbrook Farm Camping Bunk House, T01433-670235. Owned by Mr Thornley.
Upper Booth Farm, T01433-670250, www.upperboothcamping.co.uk. Ask for Mrs Hodgson.
Waterside Farm, T01433-670215. Ask for Mrs Cooper.

Eyam *p45*
££ Crown Cottage, on the main road, T01433-630858, http://crown-cottage.co.uk. The only place to stay in Eyam village. A charming white-stone cottage, formerly the old village inn, now a B&B with lovely views of the area and 4 rooms.
£ Bretton YHA, 2 miles from Eyam, T0845-371 9626, www.yha.org.uk/hostel/bretton. A small remote stone farmhouse with 18 beds.
£ Eyam YHA, Hawkhill Rd, just out of town, T0845-371 9738, www.yha.org.uk/hostel/eyam. An eccentric turreted Victorian building just up the road from the village with 60 beds, open from 1700. They also have crazy golf.

Bakewell *p46*
There are a number of B&Bs in and around Bakewell, generally family-run stone cottages. See www.bakewell-accommodation.co.uk.
££££-£££ Rutland Arms Hotel, T01629-812812, www.rutlandarmsbakewell.co.uk. A grand old establishment in the centre of Bakewell, which has played host to Wordsworth, Coleridge and Turner in the past, this is the home of the original Bakewell Pudding. It's the only hotel in the centre of Bakewell and has a welcoming restaurant serving traditional English food.
£££ Haddon House Farm, Haddon Rd just out of Bakewell, T01629-814024, http://www.great-place.co.uk. Quiet, spacious and a touch of romance with 2 luxurious double rooms.
£££-££ River Cottage, Buxton Rd, Ashford-in-the-Water, just west of Bakewell, T01629-

813327, www.rivercottageashford.co.uk.
Comfortable B&B in a house dating back to
1740 with contemporary rooms and a large
leafy garden leading down to a river.
££ Bourne House, The Park, Haddon Rd,
T01629-813274. A short stroll along the river
into town. Fairly upmarket B&B with 2
en suite rooms and private parking.
££ Croft Cottage, Coombs Rd, T01629-
814101. A gorgeous 17th-century stone
cottage with a luxury private suite in the
converted barn. Comfortable and welcoming.
££-£ Melbourne House, Buxton Rd,
T01629-815357. A private Georgian house
offering a variety of home-cooked breakfasts
and a warm welcome.

Camping and self-catering
Chatsworth Park Caravan Club Site,
T01246-582226 (Mar-Dec). In an old
walled garden.
Haddon Grove Farm, near Over Haddon
on Monyash Rd, 4 miles west of town,
T01629-812343, www.haddongrovefarm
cottages.co.uk. For camping and
family-friendly self-catering cottages.

Matlock and Matlock Bath *p47*
There are a lot of B&Bs in Matlock and the
surrounding area for a reasonable price which
cater especially for walkers. There's also a
small number of Victorian hotels in Matlock
Bath which used to attract guests who came
to the town for the water, and some still do.
£££ Old Shoulder of Mutton, West Bank,
Winster, just west of Matlock, T01629-650005,
www.oldshoulderofmutton.co.uk. Luxurious
B&B in a former pub. Rooms are full of charm
with chunky wood furniture and lovely
en suite bathrooms.
£££ The Temple Hotel, Temple
Walk, Matlock Bath, T01629-583911,
www.templehotel.co.uk. A historic stone
building with comfortable accommodation
and a bar with real ale on tap. Lord Byron
wooed one of his mistresses here, and

the restaurant is named after him. It's a
comfortable and friendly place.
£££-££ Hogkinson's Hotel, 150
South Pde, Matlock Bath, T01629-582170,
www.hodgkinsons-hotel.co.uk. A place with a
dash of Victorian elegance, terraced gardens
and a restaurant.
£££-££ Manor Farm, Dethick, just south of
Matlock, T01629-534302, www.manorfarm
dethick.co.uk. Rooms in a historic 16th-
century farm with large beams and lovely
views. Lots of character.
£££-££ Riber Hall, Riber, Matlock,
T01629-582795, www.riber-hall.co.uk.
An exceptional historic country house in
a tranquil upmarket setting, with period
furniture and exquisite detail, where you'll
receive first class treatment.
£££-££ Tinkersley Cottage, Tinkersley,
Rowsley, a few miles west of Matlock,
www.tinkersleycottage.co.uk, T07802-
494814. Stylish B&B rooms in 2 cottages
with French decor and private terrace.
££ Glendon Guest House, 7 Knowleston Pl,
Matlock, T01629-584732, www.glendon
bandb.co.uk. A Georgian B&B by the river
with 4 rooms and a relaxed atmosphere.
££ The Old Museum Guesthouse, 170
South Pde, Matlock Bath, T01629-57783. In
the centre of town, this place has 3 en suite
rooms with 4-poster beds also with views
over the river.
££-£ Farley Farm, Farley, T01629-582533,
www.farleyfarm.co.uk. A gorgeous working
country farm with log fires, a relaxing
atmosphere and home cooking, perfect
for indulging those countryside fantasies.
££-£ Fountain Villa, 86 North Pde, Matlock
Bath, T01629-56195, www.fountainvilla.co.uk.
A Georgian townhouse overlooking the
Derwent river and with period interiors.
££-£ The Old Sunday School, New St,
Matlock, T01629-583347, www.patricksthe
oldsundayschool.co.uk. If you want
something a little different from your usual
B&B try this converted ex-chapel with,

despite its history, a friendly home-from-home atmosphere.

£ Matlock Hostel, 40 Bank Rd, T01629-582983, www.youthhostelsguide.com/hostels/view/127. With charming laid-back staff, this medium-sized hostel used to be the Hydropathic Hospital. Has loads of information on the area as well as a bar. They also have information on inter-hostel walking trails which are a really good way to see the Peak District as they're only between 9 and 17 miles apart.

Camping
Middle Hills Farm Campsite, Grangemill, Matlock, T01629-650368. Cheap and quirky stone farmhouse with home-baked bread and genial hosts. You can also make friends with a potbellied pig. Camping and caravan site with toilets and showers and ½ mile from the nearest pub.

🍴 Restaurants

Buxton *p41, map p41*
There are a few pubs where you can grab a cheap meal in Buxton and several tea rooms mainly suited to day trippers.

££ The Buckingham Hotel 1 Burlington Rd, T01298-70481, www.buckinghamhotel.co.uk. Traditional English carvery menu most nights of the week, smoked salmon starters and a range of fish and vegetarian dishes too. Grilled chicken with goats' cheese and avocado, fillet steak and roast lamb are typical in this small but not unimaginative restaurant.

££ Columbine Restaurant, 7 Hall Bank, T01298-78752, www.columbine restaurant.co.uk. The town's best restaurant. Very reasonably priced for fresh local produce. There's a range of meat and fish dishes including venison in Guinness, and friendly service in a classy restaurant. Closed Sun and Tue Nov-Apr.

££ The Old Clubhouse, 3 Water St, T01298-70117, is a traditional warm pub with an open fire serving pub grub. It also has a garden for the summer months.

££ Old Hall Hotel on the Square just across from the Opera House, T01298-22841, www.oldhallhotelbuxton.co.uk. Serves English Sunday lunch-style roasts within its historic wood-panelled walls. They have a pre- and post-theatre menu and accommodation (see Where to stay).

£ The Wild Carrot, 5 Bridge St, T01298-22843, www.wildcarrot.freeserve.co.uk. Open Wed-Sun. A small licensed vegetarian café with home-cooked food. There's also a wholefood shop downstairs, open Mon-Sat.

Edale *p44*
£ The Old Nag's Head, T01433-670291, http://the-old-nags-head.co.uk. A famous walkers' pub with a garden to the rear and special walkers' meals that are high in carbohydrates.

Bakewell *p46*
There are 2 particularly good bakeries to try in the town itself.

£ The Bakewell Tart Shop and Coffee House, Matlock St, T01629-814692, www.bakewelltartshop.co.uk. Delicious variety of tarts from traditional to lemon and treacle to eat in or take away.

£ The Old Original Bakewell Pudding Shop, The Square, T01629-812193, www.bakewellpuddingshop.co.uk. Less wide-ranging but with freshly baked bread and a licensed restaurant.

Matlock *p47*
Matlock has a lot of pubs, and you'll easily find something to eat here, although characteristically for the area, it's more walkers' carbo-laden food than nouvelle cuisine.

😊 Entertainment

Buxton *p41, map p41*
The Buxton Buzz Comedy Club, at
the Pavillion Arts Centre, behind the opera
house, www.buzzcomedy.co.uk.
Buxton Opera House, Water St, T0845-127
2190, www.buxton-opera.co.uk. Regular
shows throughout the year of various genres
from book adaptations and poetry readings
to opera, ballet and popular plays.
The Pauper's Pit Theatre, in the Old Hall
Hotel, www.oldhallhotelbuxton.co.uk.
Fringe productions.

🎵 Festivals

Buxton *p41, map p41*
Jul **Buxton Military Tattoo**,
www.buxtontattoo.org.uk. Military displays
including bands, bagpipes and drums.
Jul **Buxton Festival** www.buxtonfestival.
co.uk. Festival of opera music and literature.
Jul-Aug **Gilbert and Sullivan Festival**,
www.gsfestivals.org. International artists
celebrate the one of the country's most
enduring and talented duos

🏔 What to do

Buxton *p41, map p41*
Horse riding
**Northfield Farm Riding and Trekking
Centre**, Flash, just outside Buxton, T01298-
22543, www.northfieldfarm.co.uk. Rides by
the hour or the day for all abilities. A 2-hr trek
costs £40 and it's £80 for a full day. Weekend
treks also available, accommodation on site.

Themed tours
Peak Premier Travel Tours, T01629-
636877, www.peakpremiertravel.co.uk.
Full- and half-day tours of the Peak District,
including mystery tours of the area's country
pubs. Also does pick-ups or drop offs for one-
way walks in the region.

Walking
Free guided walks run from the Hope Valley
Line stations at different dates throughout
the year. There's a good 9-mile walk from
Bamford to Edale, or an easier 7-mile walk
around **Hathersage**. All the walks start
and finish at a railway station in good
time for your train home. Ask at the
TIC for details.
Peak Tours, Glossop, T01457-851462,
www.peak-tours.com. Walking and cycling
holidays searching out the best historic
houses, wildlife and scenery. Also offers bike
hire, delivery service and accommodation.
Peak Walking Adventures, 64 Cherry Tree
Av, Belper, T07870-778585, www.peak
walking.com. Half- or full-day walks as well
as more challenging trek training days with
professional mountain guides.

Edale *p44*
Horse riding
Ladybooth Trekking Centre, T01433-
670205, www.ladybooth.co.uk. From 1-hr
treks to riding holidays, and lessons for
beginners. Farm rides for children under 12.

Bakewell *p46*
Bus tours
Visitors can now tour Buxton in a Victorian-
style tram. Tours take in the Crescent, the
Dome, the Opera House, the Market Place
and other sights before arriving at Poole's
Cavern. Ask at the TIC for details.

🚫 Transport

Hope Valley *p43*
Buses go from Castleton to **Bakewell**
5 times a day and 6 times a day to **Buxton**.
The village is 3 miles from the nearest station
in Hope, see Hope Valley Railway page 39.
The No 200 bus runs from Castleton bus
station to **Edale** station hourly from 0853
and takes 20 mins.

Cheshire

Contained within Cheshire's boundaries, which stretch from North Wales to Manchester and Derbyshire, are an inordinate number of country houses, medieval hunting estates and the small town of Prestbury, housing one of the highest proportions of millionaires per head in the country. Small wonder that a lot of Cheshire's residents have delusions of grandeur – this is an upmarket area with a very desirable postcode. Chester, the much-visited Roman city with fantastic shopping and museums, is worth a visit, as is the lush countryside that the wealthy landowners liked so much. Cheshire is a serious bit of posh amid the metropolitan areas of the Northwest, and its residents wouldn't want you to forget it.

Background

The teapot-shaped county bordered by Wales, Merseyside, Manchester, Shropshire and Derbyshire has a breadth and depth of both history and landscape. With wild hilly moorland in the east through to the western fertile plain and grassland in the south, Cheshire has a long history as an agricultural county. For nearly 500 years until 1830, it was a County Palatine, a little kingdom ruled by the Earl of Chester independently of the king. The county town, Chester, is a walled Roman town but there is also evidence of Stone Age occupation here. The county thrived during the Middle Ages with bustling market towns, and its forests became popular hunting grounds for the Earl of Chester and many kings (James I was the last known king to hunt here), before the county was decimated by plague in 1349.

But the real changes came with salt mining in the 18th and 19th centuries. The manufacturing industries coupled with canal infrastructure brought wealth to Cheshire. In 1847 the first chemical works opened up in Widnes, and the northwest of the county still has an immense mineral oil industry today. The northeast by contrast benefited from the cotton industry of Manchester, and the many mill towns were prosperous until the late 19th century, when overseas competition hit them hard. Liverpool took over from Chester as the area's major port serving Ireland, and the county's fortunes changed again. Its shape has changed over the years, as you might imagine, and the most recent change has been the loss of the Wirral Peninsula in the north to Merseyside.

These days, Cheshire retains many small historic market towns while accommodating some of the urban sprawl of Merseyside and Manchester, and the far less picturesque but immensely valuable chemical works still bring in the money in Runcorn.

Chester → *For listings, see pages 61-63.*

Chester is a walled Roman city on the Welsh borders, and the Romans still rule the roost here today. Don't be surprised if you see the odd centurion or two sitting around having a coffee in one of the many cafés in the centre of town – as you'll realize within five minutes of being here, tourism is the main industry. Despite the Roman theme, your first impressions are likely to be of the beautiful black-and-white Tudor-style architecture, particularly the Rows, the half-timbered shopping precincts unique to Chester. While browsing the many shops, your ears will be assailed by any number of regional accents, buskers and the odd gabble of Welsh – the language still thrives a couple of miles away across the border. Walking around the walls, taking a boat trip on the Dee and enjoying the historic pubs after a shopping spree around the Rows are some of the best ways to spend your day here.

Arriving in Chester
Getting there Chester is well-linked by motorways, rail and bus routes to the rest of Britain although public transport around Cheshire as a whole is less user-friendly. **Manchester Airport** (see page 19) is 40 minutes away from Chester, on the M56 and M53, for international and domestic flights. **Liverpool John Lennon Airport** (see page 65) is also 40 minutes away by road. There are high-speed rail services from London Euston and Paddington to Crewe and Chester, also from Glasgow on the West Coast Main Line. It's

also easy to get here from Manchester's Piccadilly and Oxford Road stations and Birmingham New Street. The train station is a 15-minute walk from the centre. The bus station is on Delamere Street for all regional and national buses. Be warned that the local buses in this area aren't particularly direct or reliable. You can get to North Wales from here by bus and around Cheshire, but you'll need to check the timetables closely. **National Express** ① T08705-808080, www.nationalexpress.co.uk, runs coach services around Britain, and **Traveline Northwest** ① T0871-200 2233, www.traveline-northwest.co.uk, has further information on local transport.

Chester

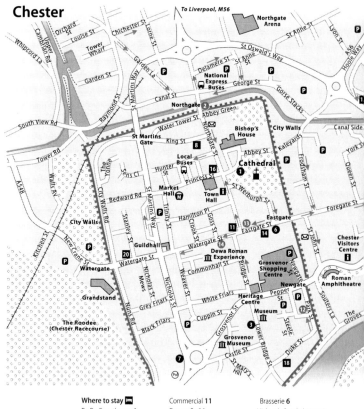

Where to stay	Commercial **11**	Brasserie **6**
Ba Ba Guesthouse **1**	Dragonfly **20**	Hickory's Smokehouse **4**
Cheltenham Lodge **2**	Mill **17**	Michael Caines @ Abode **5**
Cheshire Cat **5**	Recorder **18**	Olive Tree **8**
Chester Brooklands B&B **15**		Red House **9**
Chester Grosvenor **14**	**Restaurants**	Refectory **1**
Chester Town House **8**	The Garden @ Oddfellows **3**	Sticky Walnut **10**
Coach House Inn **16**	Grosvenor Hotel	

Getting around It only takes 20 minutes to walk from one side of Chester to the other, and going by foot is your only option as the centre of town is pedestrianized. Naturally, there are plenty of well-signposted car parks, mainly to the north of the town and a number of park and ride options at the far edges of the city.

Tourist information Just outside the city walls to the southwest of the city is the excellent **Chester Visitor Centre** ① *Town Hall Sq, T01244-401796, www.visitchester.com, Mon-Sat 0900-1730, Sun 1000-1700.* They can help with accommodation and transport bookings as well as tickets for attractions, city sightseeing tours, boat trips, heritage tours and guided walking tours. There's also a shop on site with gifts and local crafts. The websites www.chestertourist.com and www.chester.com have lots of useful information for visitors.

Background

Archaeologists have found evidence of human occupation in Chester since the Stone Age, but it really came to power as a trading settlement for the Romans from AD 1 until AD 410. The Romans named it Deva, after the goddess of the river Dee and it was one of the finest strategic outposts in England because of its proximity to the Welsh borders and its harbour. Roman relics are scattered around the city today, highlights being a half-excavated amphitheatre, which would have sat around 6000 people, and the Grosvenor Museum, which contains the greatest number of Roman tombstones to be found outside Rome; they were discovered underpinning the city walls in the 19th century. In the 13th and 14th centuries Chester developed as a port, mainly for trade with Ireland, and was a military base for incursions against the Welsh. The Rows date back to around this time: half-timbered galleries on two levels, which were named after the merchants trading on each one, for example Pepper Alley, Fish Shambles and Ironmongers' Row. Those that remain today are mainly Victorian reconstructions in the derided "mock-Tudor" style, but they are unique in England, and in some the medieval vaulted undercrofts remain.

Pubs & bars 🍸
Albion Inn **12**
Alexander's Jazz
  Bar Restaurant **2**
Old Boot Inn **13**
Watergate's **14**

Chester suffered greatly in the Civil War of 1642-1646, when it chose to support the wrong side. Cromwell's men besieged the city for two years until starvation forced it to surrender; it had the last laugh, though, when Charles II came to the throne in 1660, bringing the wealthy back to his loyal town.

Today Chester remains a historic town and has yet to become a museum town. It prides itself on its history but also houses many businesses and still operates as a modern urban centre. However, of late, shopping outlets such as the Trafford Centre in Manchester and Cheshire Oaks in Ellesmere Port have stifled smaller shops, which are quietly closing down along the Rows. For those living in the small market towns in Wales and Cheshire though, Chester is still a place to come to find the best variety of shops in one place.

Places in Chester

Starting at the Visitor Centre at the town hall, walk under the 14th-century archway to the left of the cathedral into Abbey Square and through the northwest corner to find the **city wall**. Walking along the wall away from town will take you to the **Northgate** with its canals and locks behind it.

This is the beginning of a 40-minute walk into town which takes in most of the sights of Chester. To your left, the **cathedral** ① *T01244-324756, www.chestercathedral.com, Mon-Sat 0900-1700, Sun 1300-1600, donation*, stands where there has been a church since AD 907. The cloisters are very atmospheric, and it has a very good information trail including a manuscript of Handel's *Messiah*, which he practised here en route to Ireland.

Next, the **Eastgate**, once the main entrance to the city is now a bridge over the main shopping street, Eastgate Street, with the second most photographed clock in England after the Great Clock on the Elizabethan Tower of Westminster (Big Ben), commemorating 60 years of Queen Victoria's reign. Walking on, you reach **Newgate** from which there is a view over the **Roman amphitheatre** to the left and the Chester visitor centre beyond it. It's not that impressive and has only been half excavated but held 6000-7000 spectators in its day. Beyond it is **Grosvenor Park**, a local beauty spot and ideal for a picnic.

Just beyond Newgate is the river, reached easily if you go down **the wishing steps**. Folklore has it that if you run up and down and then up again without drawing breath, your wish will come true. There aren't all that many of them, but the steps are uneven in depth, which makes running up and down them treacherous.

Walking from here into town along the walls will take you to the Southgate, known locally as **Bridgegate** as it's opposite the 14th-century bridge out of town. Continuing round on the walls for a further 10 minutes will take you to the **Roodee Racecourse** ① *T01244-304610, www.chester-races.co.uk*, Britain's oldest. There are racing festivals at various points throughout the summer, and the horses, unusually, run anti-clockwise. Otherwise, from Bridgegate you can head straight up the street into town to shop in the Rows. A number of the shops have interesting histories, for example **The Bear at the Billet**, just by Bridgegate on the left, Chester's oldest timber-frame house, and on Bridge Street Row, **Booklands** bookshop, which has a beautiful vaulted medieval crypt.

The **Grosvenor Museum** ① *T01244-972197, Mon-Sat 1030-1700, Sun 1300-1600, free*, is a bit dusty but has some interesting exhibits if you want to find out more about the town's history. Bringing the history alive more successfully is the **Dewa Roman Experience** ① *Pierpoint Lane, just off Bridge St, T01244-343407, www.dewaromanexperience.co.uk, daily 0900-1700*, a museum with lots of hands-on features.

Around Cheshire → *For listings, see pages 61-63.*

Ellesmere Port
Seven miles north of Chester, Ellesmere Port is the site of the popular **British Waterways Museum** ① *South Pier Rd, T0151-355 5017, daily 1000-1700, £6.50, concessions £5.50, child £4.50, shop and café on site.* As well as running boat trips, it shows you just how important messing about on the river has been in this area over the years and is actually very interesting. It's only a 10-minute walk from the Ellesmere Port railway station.

Macclesfield and around
The borough of Macclesfield in north Cheshire is the largest district in the county, comprising Alderley Edge, Knutsford, Poynton and Wilmslow, and is easily the most affluent. Accessible on the London–Manchester intercity rail link or from the M6, 'Macc' (as it's known to residents) is primarily known for its 18th- and 19th-century silk industry. At that time it was the greatest silk-weaving town in England. There are three museums dedicated to the town's silk industry, collectively known as the **Macclesfield Silk Museums** ① *T01625-613210, www.silkmacclesfield.org.uk, Mon-Sat 1000-1500, 1 site £3.50, child £3, 2 sites £6, child £5.25, 3 sites £9, child £8.* The **Silk Industry Museum**, on Park Lane, follows the journey through the industrial process of silk making and has lots of hands-on exhibits. Next door, **Paradise Mill** is a working Victorian silk mill where you can take a tour to give you a taste of life in the early 1900s. The museum at the **Heritage Centre** on Roe Street follows the lives of the silk industry creators and has a silk costume collection and silk merchant shop with products by local artists. It tells the story of the town, whose football team are still known as the Silkmen.

Starting at the top of Macclesfield by Tesco's are 11 miles of an old railway line, the **Middlewood Way**, which has been made into a footpath. It runs parallel to the Macclesfield Canal along grassland and links up with the towpath as an ideal place for a Sunday walk or bike ride. A walk to **Bollington** along the path is easy and rewarding as this little country town a couple of miles from Macclesfield has some nice old pubs.

The B5087 from Macclesfield to Alderley Edge turns north to the picturesque village of **Prestbury**. The river Bollin runs through this historic town complete with half-timbered Tudor buildings, and it's no wonder that so many affluent people have chosen to live around here. It's known in the area for being the village with the most millionaires per mile in the county, if not the country. From Prestbury you can wiggle round the village roads past Mottram St Andrews to **Alderley Edge**. The town itself is nothing special, but just before it is an area of outstanding natural beauty. Take your time to stop for a walk to the **Edge**, 250 acres of sandstone ridge with views out over the Cheshire Plain as far as the Peak District. It's a magical place that inspired Alan Garner's children's book, *The Weirdstone of Brisingamen*; Bronze Age remains and a beacon that was lit to warn of the Spanish Armada add to the romance.

Knutsford
A couple of miles west of Macclesfield on the A537 is the small town of Knutsford. It's all that you would expect of a Cheshire town: historic chocolate box cottages, a plethora of antiques shops and exclusive restaurants and a large country mansion in the background. If it feels like you've walked into a 19th-century novel, well, that's because you have.

Elizabeth Gaskell based her novels of the industrial revolution here, including *Cranford*. From the train station, the view down the main street, King Street, is dominated by the GMT, or **Gaskell Memorial Tower**. Built in 1907 to the memory of the novelist, it's quite an ugly thing with the names of her novels marked along it, as well as a bust of the author. Next to it is the architecturally more interesting belle époque restaurant, formerly the civic centre, which is one of a number of eccentric Italianate buildings in Knutsford. **RH Watt**, a Manchester glovemaker, brought back these ideals of architecture from his travels through southern Europe. Drury Lane at the end of King Street has a number of examples of his buildings, including the Ruskin Rooms, after the painter who inspired Watt, now offices.

The **Knutsford Heritage Centre** ① *90A King St, T01565-650506, www.knutsford heritage.co.uk, Mon-Fri 1330-1600, Sat 1200-1600, Sun 1400-1630, free,* just beside **Jumpers**, was a 19th-century smithy and has a permanent exhibition about the town upstairs, including a video of its unusual Mayday parade. They have plenty of information about historic trails round the town and cheerfully answer all enquiries.

Following the blue heritage plaques down the street, you will eventually come to the entrance to **Tatton Park** ① *(NT), T01625-534400, www.tattonpark.org.uk, park, Apr-Oct daily 1000-1900, Nov-Mar Tue-Sun 1000-1700, £5 for cars, free for walkers, mansion, gardens, Tudor old hall and farm (varied opening hours, see the website), £10 for all 3 attractions, child £5.* The home of the Egerton family, this National Trust property has 1000 acres of land as well as a Georgian mansion, Japanese gardens and the Tudor old hall, which takes you through 450 years of history from the 15th century to the 1950s. On a nice day, a walk in the park is superb – and free – and you can see herds of red deer up close, as well as numerous birds. It's just a shame that Manchester Airport is so close, as the jet engines shatter your calm every now and again. Be warned: a walk from the gates to the hall itself is pretty exhausting and you really need a car or at least a bike to reach it.

Lyme Park

Take the A523 from Macclesfield to Hazel Grove and then the A6 to High Lane and you'll find **Lyme Park** ① *(NT), T01663-762023, hall and gardens, Apr-Oct Fri-Tue 1300-1700, park, Apr-Oct daily 0800-2030, Nov-Mar 0800-1800, free for walkers, £11, child £5.50, you can also reach the park by train and a short walk from Disley station.* In the borough of Stockport, it's the largest country house in Cheshire. With Ionic pillars, Greek marbles and an Elizabethan drawing room, the 16th-century house itself is very grand and not surprisingly frequently used as a backdrop for period dramas, including the BBC adaptation of *Pride and Prejudice*, where a dripping Colin Firth, as Mr Darcy, took a swim in the lake. Walks around the grounds along a number of well-marked trails are free and worth the effort. From the car park you can easily walk to **The Cage**, the folly at the top of the nearest hill from where the ladies of the house used to watch the hunt. You can see the Peak District from the top of the hill and the many red and fallow deer across the estate. More gruesomely, the lower part of the cage was used to jail poachers.

Cheshire listings

For hotel and restaurant price codes and other relevant information, see pages 9-12.

🛏 Where to stay

Chester *p55, map p56*

There are plenty of places to stay in Chester to suit every budget, which is atypical of Cheshire in general, so it's a good place to base yourself if you're exploring this area. Around the station are a huge number of guesthouses and hotels of a similar standard. Hoole Rd is also good for budget B&Bs, as is Hough Green on the opposite side of town.

££££-£££ The Chester Grosvenor Eastgate St, T01244-324024, www.chestergrosvenor.com. Bang in the centre of town, this place is owned by the Duke of Westminster and is one of the plushest hotels in the area. It is grand and traditional with leather armchairs and 4-poster beds. Indulgences include a spa, plush restaurants and afternoon tea.

£££ Coach House Inn, 39 Northgate St, T01244-351900, www.coachhouse chester.co.uk. Large, comfortable en suite rooms and a good restaurant attached.

£££ Commercial Hotel, St Peter's Churchyard, T01244-320749, www.thecommercialhotelchester.co.uk. A country hotel-style place with ivy growing up the walls and individual service, 6 rooms and a relaxed atmosphere.

£££ Dragonfly Hotel, 94 New Crane St, (Watergate St), T01244-346740, www.hotel dragonfly.com. Boutique hotel in a Georgian townhouse offering modern luxury en suite rooms with Wi-Fi, flatscreen TV and fluffy bathrobes.

£££-££ Recorder Hotel, right in the centre of Chester at 19 City Walls, overlooking the River Dee, T01244-326580, www.recorder hotel.co.uk. A stately guesthouse with individually designed bedrooms (12 guest rooms named after the signs of the zodiac), it also has romantic 4-poster and Victorian beds and the location is perfect.

££ Albion Inn, Park St, T01244-340345, www.albioninnchester.co.uk. Victorian corner pub with memorabilia commemorating WWI. Cosy bedrooms have en suite bathroom and there's good food served downstairs.

££ Ba Ba Guest House, 65 Hoole Rd, T01244-315047, www.babaguesthouse.co.uk. An elegant Victorian townhouse; it's one of the most friendly and welcoming B&Bs in town.

££ Cheltenham Lodge, 58 Hoole Rd, T01244-346767 www.bedandbreakfastinchester.co.uk. 5 spacious bedrooms with period features and en suite bathrooms, Wi-Fi. Off-street parking.

££ Cheshire Cat, Whitchurch Rd, Christleton, T01244-332200, www.vintageinn.co.uk/the cheshirecatchristleton. Slightly out of town, a country hotel with 14 rooms and a homely feel.

££ Chester Town House, 23 King St, T01244-350021, www.chestertownhouse.co.uk. A comfortable 17th-century guesthouse with a family feel to it.

££ Mill Hotel and Spa, Milton St near the station, T01244-350035, www.millhotel.com. A new modern hotel that used to be an old corn mill. Now with state-of-the-art gym and spa complex.

££-£ Chester Brooklands B&B, 8 Newton Lane, T01244-348856, www.chester-bandb.co.uk. Smart B&B with spacious rooms with sash windows and Victorian fireplaces. Off-street parking.

Knutsford *p59*

££ The Cross Keys Hotel, King St, T01565-750404, www.crosskeysknutsford.com. Offers accommodation in the stables of the former 18th-century coaching inn with plenty of character and wooden beams and no horses.

££ Tattondale Farm, Tatton Park, Ashley Rd, T01565-654692. A working farm in the grounds of Tatton Park (see page 60) itself.

Chester *p55, map p56*

£££ The Brasserie at the **Grosvenor Hotel**, Eastgate St, T01244-324024, www.chester grosvenor.com. Upmarket hotel restaurant serving French food in an elegant setting. Pop in for traditional English afternoon tea if you can't afford a meal.

£££ Olive Tree, Green Bough Hotel, 60 Hoole Rd, T01244-320779, www.chester greenboughhotel.com. With stylish Italian decor and discreet service, this is fine dining at its best, with canapés and pre-dinner drinks served in the lounge or rooftop garden followed by elegant mains. Or come for afternoon tea. There's also a cookery school.

£££-££, The Garden @ Oddfellows, 20 Lower Bridge St, T01244-895700, www.oddfellowschester.com/dine. Mediterranean-inspired menu with the option to dine in the garden if it's warm enough. The emphasis is on casual sophistication with menus to share or à la carte.

£££-££ Sticky Walnut, 11 Charles St, T01244-400400, www.stickywalnut.com. Modern restaurant with a bohemian feel. Menu includes delicious British, French and Italian dishes with home-made pasta and bread.

££ Hickory's Smokehouse, The Groves, T01244-404000, www.hickorys.co.uk. Authentic American barbecue complete with buffalo wings, slow-cooked ribs, popcorn, milkshakes and Brooklyn lager. Overlooking the River Dee.

££ Red House, Great Boughton, east of the centre, T01244-320088, www.red housechester.com. On the banks of the Dee, this modern restaurant has floor-to-ceiling windows so you can look out over the river as you dine. It's a great place for a relaxed Sunday roast or hearty main.

££-£ Joseph Benjamin, 140 North Gate St, T01244-34429, www.josephbenjamin.co.uk.

A restaurant, bar and deli adjacent to the city walls. Food is seasonal, full of flavour and beautifully presented. Also offers snacks and sandwiches from the deli.

£ Refectory Café, Chester Cathedral, T01244-500964, www.chestercathedral.com. Mon-Sat 0930-1630, Sun 1200-1600. A very cheap and wholesome affair, seating on benches in what feels like a school canteen but with much nicer home-made snacks.

Knutsford *p59*

There are a lot of upmarket places to dine here on King St alongside a number of pubs with reasonable lunches.

££ Belle Epoque, 60 King St, T01565-632661, www.thebelleepoque.com. An award-winning French restaurant with starched white tablecloths and an air of exclusivity.

Chester *p55, map p56*

One of the best ways of soaking up the atmosphere is a lunch in one of the city's many low-beamed pubs, although occasionally they're a little too tourist-orientated with their spurious tales of ghosts and the like. Most stop serving lunch after 1400.

Albion Inn, Park St, T01244-340345, www.albioninnchester.co.uk. A great stopping point along the walls just after Newgate. It serves outstanding pub grub and has a warming log fire in winter.

Alexander's Jazz Bar Restaurant, Rufus Court, T01244-340 0050, www.alexanders live.com. Live music venue with jazz, blues, soul, roots and rock. Stand-up comedy on Sat. Also does good food.

The Old Boot Inn, 9 Eastgate St, T01244-314540. The oldest surviving pub in Chester, with traditional decor and oak beams and pub lunches. 14 roundheads were killed in the back room.

Watergate's Wine Bar, 11-13 Watergate St, T01244-320515. Recommended for its candlelit crypt dating from 1120 with nooks and crannies to sit in and a friendly, young and trendy atmosphere.

⚠ What to do

Chester *p55, map p56*
Guided walks
Guided walks around town can be arranged through the tourist office, some with guides dressed in full Roman gear leading children whooping around the streets, and there's also a brilliant ghost hunter tour (every Thu, Fri and Sat from outside the town hall at 1930, Jun-Oct). This takes you past a number of pubs where spirits have been spotted over the years by those drinking too much of the same, and along the walls where a centurion is supposed to roam. Contact the TIC for further details.

⊖ Transport

Chester *p55, map p56*
Bus
Long distance There are 10 **National Express** coach services daily to **London** (6 hrs), 8 to **Birmingham** (2 hrs), 6 to **Cardiff** (5 hrs), 8 to **Gatwick** (8 hrs), 8 to **Liverpool** (1 hr), 6 to Manchester and **Manchester airport** (1 hr). For **Edinburgh** there are 4 services a day (11 hrs) and buses run to **Glasgow** twice daily (7 hrs).

Car
Avis, 128 Brook St, T01244-311463, www.avis.co.uk; **Budget**, The Bridgegate, Lower Bridge St, T01244-313431, www.budget.co.uk; **Hertz**, Trafford St, T01244-374705, www.hertz.co.uk; **Europcar**, 143 Brook St, T01244-312893, www.europcar.co.uk.

Train
Central Trains, www.centraltrains.co.uk, run from Chester to **Birmingham** (2 hrs) and **London Euston** (4 hrs). **First Northwestern** run the stopping service from Chester to **Manchester** via Knutsford (1 hr 15 mins) and various services into Wales including to **Holyhead** for the boat to **Dublin** (1½ hrs).

Knutsford *p59*
Bus
Buses go to **Macclesfield** hourly from here, for further information contact www.traveline.info.

Car
Knutsford is on the old Liverpool–London road, the A50, and is 10 miles from Manchester Airport, 37 miles from Liverpool and 15 miles from Manchester.

Train
Trains to **Manchester** go hourly, just after the ½ hr and to **Chester** in the opposite direction just before it.

Liverpool

Built around the docks and the River Mersey, Liverpool is essentially a small city with the vibrant blend of cultures that its history as a major port has produced. Once known for its scallies, shell suits and curly perms, the city has transformed immeasurably over the last 10 years.

In 2004 the whole of the waterfront and docks area was designated as a UNESCO World Heritage Site, and in 2008 it won the title of European Capital of Culture. As a result, the city was given a makeover and the skyline now is now dotted with shiny new buildings sitting comfortably alongside its many handsome listed ones. Derelict warehouses have been converted into cafés, shops and apartments, and the city boasts an exceptional modern art scene, world-class museums and, of course, the Beatles.

You could be forgiven for thinking that Liverpool has stood still after the demise of the four cheeky scousers: through the Cavern Quarter to the Albert Dock you'll find tours and trips to satisfy the worst of Beatlemaniacs. The overdose of Beatles culture can be righted with a trip to the Ropewalks area, throbbing with clubs and bars and perfect for a hard day's night.

Arriving in Liverpool → *For listings, see pages 74-80.*

Getting there
Air Liverpool John Lennon Airport ⓘ *Speke, 9 miles southeast of the city centre, T0871-521 8484, www.liverpoolairport.com*, is well served from Europe and the UK by budget airlines including easyJet and Ryanair. The airport has currency exchange facilities and ATMs in the main terminal, as well as a helpful tourist information desk (open 0600-2000). There are excellent public transport links into central Liverpool and to a number of major towns and cities in the area. The **Arriva Airlink 500** bus runs to the city centre, including London Road (for National Express coach connections) and Lime Street Station (for onward train connections). There are also buses to the rail terminal at Liverpool South Parkway, two miles away, which connects with the main train line into the city. A taxi from the airport to the city centre costs about £15; contact **Mersey Cabs** ⓘ *T0151-298 2222, www.merseycabs.co.uk*. See also **Traveline** ⓘ *T0871-200 2233, www.traveline.co.uk*.

Bus National Express ⓘ *T08705-808080, www.nationalexpress.co.uk*, buses run from the Norton Street Station, 300 m north of the Lime Street train station. There are services to all major UK cities and towns including London (5½ hours), Manchester (1¼ hours), Birmingham (three hours) and Newcastle (seven hours).

Car Liverpool is 35 miles from Manchester on the M62 and M60, 215 miles from London and 102 miles from Birmingham on the M6. From the M6 follow the M56 or M62.

Ferry Services between Liverpool (Birkenhead) and Belfast and Dublin are operated by **Stena Line Irish Sea Ferries** ⓘ *www.stenaline.co.uk*, and between Liverpool and Douglas by the **Isle of Man Steam Packet Company** ⓘ *T0151-242 5180, www.steam-packet.com*. The **Liverpool Cruise Terminal** ⓘ *Gate 2, Princes Parade, T0151-233 2008, www.cruise-liverpool.com*, completed in 2012, is on the waterfront and sees a couple of ships a month.

Train Liverpool's main station is Lime Street, well signposted just north of the centre, which has good train links with most towns and cities and has hourly connections with London (three hours) and Manchester (45 minutes). The **First Transpennine Express** ⓘ *www.tpexpress.co.uk*, links Liverpool with Manchester. ▶▶ *See Transport, page 80.*

Getting around
Finding your way around Liverpool isn't too difficult. It's a manageable size and you can orientate yourself easily by looking up to the Radio City tower, St John's Beacon, or looking out towards the Royal Liver building and the docks. The Pier Head and the Albert Dock are a 15-minute walk from the centre, or two minutes in a taxi or a bus, running from Queen Square bus station.

The bus network is managed by **Merseytravel** ⓘ *T0151-236 7676, www.merseytravel.gov.uk*, with two main city centre bus terminals: Liverpool ONE and Queen Square. The local rail system is run by **Merseyrail** ⓘ *T0151-702 2071, www.merseyrail.org*, and links the four city stations: Lime Street; Central (for Ropewalks); James Street (for Albert Dock); and Moorfields (for the Western Approaches Museum) with greater Merseyside. The cross-Mersey ferry (£1.35, child £1.05) for Woodside and Seacombe departs from Pier

Head Ferry Terminal, next to the Liver Building to the north of Albert Dock. The **Saveaway** ticket allows unlimited offpeak travel on bus, trains and ferries within Merseyside; tickets are available from post offices and shops or the Paradise Street bus station.

Tourist information
The main tourist office is at the **Albert Dock Visitor Centre TIC** ① *Anchor Courtyard, T0151-707 0729, www.albertdock.com, Apr-Dec 1000-1760, Oct-Mar 1000-1700.* They can book transport and accommodation for you. There are also TICs at St George's Hall, John Lennon Airport and Southport. Another useful point of contact is the website and telephone helpline of **Visit Liverpool** ① *T0151-233 2008, www.visitliverpool.com.* The council website, www.liverpool.gov.uk also has some useful information. The local newspapers *The Daily Post* and *Liverpool Echo* provide the regional news for Liverpool and Merseyside. The *Metro* appears at stations in the morning, a freebie for commuters with club and event listings inside.

Background

On the Mersey estuary three miles from the Irish sea, Liverpool has a long tradition of seafaring. Founded in the 10th century, the small community became a town in 1207 when King John granted it a charter, and it grew slowly through the Middle Ages as a fishing port. The first dock was built in Liverpool in 1715, and it soon outranked London. As with Manchester, Liverpool really came to power in the 18th century as a result of trade. It was officially made a city as the growing population and industry drew in workers from all over the country and the town expanded along the docks. Irish, Welsh and Scots were attracted by the economic opportunities or came as refugees from the poverty in their own areas.

By 1830 and the introduction of the railways, Liverpool was linked with Manchester and its growing cotton trade. With the Cheshire salt fields to the south and the coal fields of Lancashire to the north, the transport network of the Mersey was a vital link in the trade of the Northwest. Its location also made trade possible with the West Indies and the Americas, and it became the most important port in the empire during this period. This status was, however, underpinned with a darker history. Liverpool was also Europe's main slave port, trading goods from Merseyside for slaves in West Africa.

From 1845 to 1848 the Potato Famine in Ireland brought in more immigrants than ever before, many hoping for a passage to America. A large proportion stayed in Liverpool, unable to afford the boat over and the city has a rich Irish heritage today.

After the Second World War the city fell into decline as both an export and a passenger port. Trade slowed down and unemployment was rife as airlines began to replace boats. But the city soon became famous for another reason besides workers' strikes. In the 1960s, Allan Ginsberg described the city as "the cultural centre of the universe" and with good reason. The place was buzzing with music and talent. In that same year, the Beatles put Liverpool firmly on the map. The city has also produced two prime ministers amid myriad entertainers and sportsmen and its contribution to England's pop culture has been assured with sitcoms, singers and footballers aplenty.

After being nominated as the European Capital of Culture for 2008, Liverpool saw EU grants come flooding in and has experienced the most significant regeneration to its city centre since the post-war reconstruction.

24 hours in Liverpool

Begin your day with a greasy fry-up in **Ye Cracke** off Hardman Street, an old Lennon hang-out that's popular with students. Then head for the **Walker Gallery** to spend your morning in the city's best and most extensive art gallery.

From there you can wander down to the **Cavern Quarter** to snoop around the street that was swinging in the sixties, and then jump on a bus to the **Albert Dock** for lunch in one of its waterside cafés or restaurants. Spend the afternoon looking round one of the excellent museums plus **The Beatles Story** before heading to **Hope Street** for a smart dinner. Round off your day in the **Ropewalks**, which has enough trendy bars and clubs to see you through till morning.

Places in Liverpool

Albert Dock

The Albert Dock, once the main quayside for the influential port in the 19th century, is now the city's main tourist attraction. You'll no longer see sacks of spices and exotic produce in the complex but some impressive museums telling the story of the city, from the slave trade through to the Beatles, amid cafés and a few touristy shops.

Just before you enter the Albert Dock along the Wapping Road that runs parallel to the dock, you'll see two modern sculptures, both bright yellow. One is the *Yellow Submarine*, cheery and recognizable from the cartoon, welcoming you to the city's biggest and best Beatles museum (see below), inside the dock. The other is *SuperLambBanana*. It's basically a giant 18-ft yellow lamb morphing into a banana, the work of Japanese artist Taro Chiezo. It's a weird sight, set against the background of 19th-century warehouses, and it's one of many modern street sculptures you'll see in the city.

The entry point to the Albert Dock at Britannia Pavilion blasts a selection of Beatles' hits at you luring you into the unmissable **Beatles Story** ① *T0151-709 1963, www.beatles story.com, Apr-Oct daily 0900-1900, Nov-Mar daily 1000-1600, £12.95, concessions, child £7, ticket valid for 48 hrs.* Walk through mocked-up streets of Liverpool and Hamburg, including a fake Cavern, and check out Lennon's white 'Imagine' piano. This is the city's finest tribute to the Fab Four from beginning to end. Set in the basement vaults it's a must if you're a fan. You'll be singing harmonies all day long and you can visit the gift shop stuffed full of memorabilia if you don't fancy paying the entry fee.

Walking through the docks around the square to the right, you'll find the TIC in the Atlantic Pavilion. On Hartley Quay the **Merseyside Maritime Museum** ① *T0151-478 4499, www.liverpoolmuseums.org.uk, daily 1000-1700, free,* incorporates the **National Museum of the UK Border Force (Siezed!)**, in the basement, and the **International Slavery Museum** on the third floor. Seized! has plenty of interactive features allowing you to experience a-day-in-the-life-of a customs officer including intriguing displays on smuggling and crime fighting. There's also a *Titanic* gallery. If you don't have time to visit any other attraction in Liverpool, make sure you don't miss the deeply moving slavery museum. The exhibition, opened by Maya Angelou in 1992, explores this area of history in a personal and affecting way.

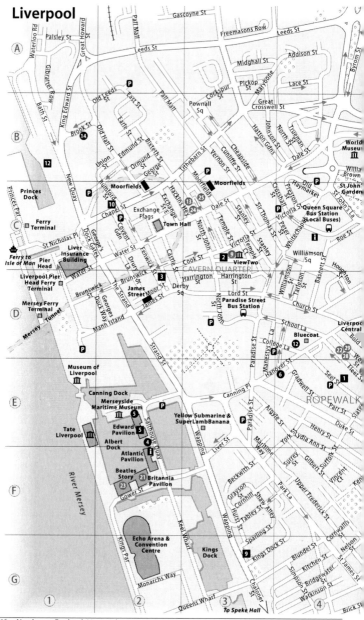

Liverpool

Gascoyne St
Freemasons Row
Leeds St
Paisley St
Waterloo Rd
Great Howard St
Gibralter Row
Pall Mall
Leeds St
Midghall St
Addison St
Pickop St
Marybone
Lace St
Cockspur St
Great Crosswell St
Pownall Sq
North John St
Hatton Gdns
Cheapside
Cunliffe St
Vernon St
Dale St
Truman St
Old Leeds St
East St
Pall Mall
Moorfields
Brook St
14
Union St
Edmund St
Ormand St
Bixteth St
George St
Tithebarn St
Johnson St
World Museum
William Brown
St John Garden
New Quay
12
Princes Dock
Rumford St
Chapel St
Moorfields
10
Exchange Flags
Covent Gdn
Town Hall
Moorfields
Hackins Hey
Exchange St
Dale St
Stanley St
Victoria St
Sir Thomas St
Preston St
Haymarket
Crosshall St
Old Haymarket
St John's La
Queen Square Bus Station (Local Buses)
Roe St
Ferry Terminal
Princes Par
St Nicholas Pl
Georges Dock Gates
Water St
Fenwick St
Castle St
North John St
Cook St
Temple St
Stanley St
Whitechapel
Peter St
Williamson Sq
i
Houghton St
Williamson Sq
Ferry to Isle of Man
Pier Head
Liver Insurance Building
13 25
24
2 ViewTwo
CAVERN QUARTER
Liverpool Pier Head Ferry Terminal
Water St
Drury La
Brunswick St
3
Harrington St
Harrington St
Victoria St
Sir Thomas St
Basnett St
Mersey Ferry Terminal
Brunswick St
James Street
Moor St
Derby Sq
Lord St
North John St
Paradise Street Bus Station
Church St
Liverpool Central
Mersey Tunnel
Georges Dock Way
Mann Island
James St
School La
Bluecoat
Bold St
Museum of Liverpool
Strand St
Canning Pl
Paradise St
Manesty's La
Hanover St
College La
12
6
Gradwell St
22 29
28
We
Fleet St
Steel St
1
Canning Dock
Merseyside Maritime Museum
Salthouse Quay
Yellow Submarine & SuperLambBanana
Wapping
Paradise St
Argyle St
Parr St
ROPEWALK
Duke St
5
Tate Liverpool
Edward Pavilion
5
Albert Dock
4
Atlantic Pavilion
Liver St
Maritime Way
Beckwith St
York St
Surrey St
Gilbert St
Henry St
Lydia Ann St
Suffolk St
Vincent St
Beatles Story
23
21
Britannia Pavilion
Gower St
Grayson St
Cornhill
Shaw Alley
Park La
Upper Frederick St
Cornwallis St
River Mersey
Kings Par
Keel Wharf
Wapping
Tabley St
Hurst St
Liver Dock St
Sparling St
Blundel St
Nelson St
St James St
Echo Arena & Convention Centre
Kings Dock
9
Kitchen St
Bridgewater St
Simpson St
Watkinson St
Monarchs Way
Queens Wharf
Chaloner St
To Speke Hall

150 metres
150 yards

Where to stay 🛏

Aachen **4** *D/E6*
Base2Stay **1** *E4*
Blenheim Lakeside **5** *E2*
Embassie Hostel **6** *G6*
Hard Days Night **2** *C3*
Heywood House **3** *D2*
Hope Street **7** *F6*
Indigo **10** *C2*
International Inn **8** *E6*
Liverpool YHA **9** *G3*
Malmaison **12** *B1*

Restaurants 🍴

60 Hope St **1** *F6*
Blue Bar & Grill **4** *E2*
Café Tabac **18** *E5*
Egg Café **3** *D/E5*
Eureka **7** *E6*
Gusto **5** *E2*
Hannah's **2** *E6*
Hanover Street Social **6** *E4*
HOST **8** *F6*
LEAF **10** *E5*
London Carriage
  Works **11** *F6*
Lunya **12** *D4*
Panoramic 34 **14** *B1*
Pushka **15** *F6*
The Quarter **16** *F6*

Pubs, bars & clubs 🍸

Alma de Cubac **17** *E5*
Attic Bar **20** *E5*
Baa Bar **22** *D4*
Cavern Club **9** *C3*
Circo **21** *F2*
Fly in the Loaf **22** *E6*
G Bar **13** *C3*
Garlands **25** *C3*
Korova **21** *E4*
Modo **28** *D4*
PanAm **23** *F2*
Philharmonic **19** *E6*
Revolution **29** *D4*
Thomas Rigby's **24** *C3*
Zanzibar Club **25** *E5*

Magical Mystery Tour

In 1960 four local Scouse lads changed the face of music forever. Hailing from Liverpool, John, Paul, George and Pete Best, soon to be replaced by Ringo Starr, spent the 60s singing about the places they'd remember all their lives, from Strawberry Fields to Penny Lane. Some places have changed and some remain the same, but here's a few of the places you can visit:

The Beatles Story, Albert Dock, T0151-709 1963. They've got the white *Imagine* piano on loan from George Michael in this museum, as well as a complete history of the band from Hamburg to the present day.

20 Forthlin Road, Speke, T0151-427 7231. Paul McCartney's childhood home and the kitchen where he and Lennon wrote *Love Me Do*. Now owned by the National Trust.

Mendips, 251 Menlove Avenue, where Lennon lived with his aunt until he was 23, has recently been bought by Yoko Ono and donated to the National Trust. Tours leave from the Albert Dock and Speke Hall.

The Cavern Club, Cavern Quarter, T0871-222 1957. The Cavern witnessed 300 performances from the Beatles here in the 1960s as well as a final gig of the century from Paul McCartney in December 1999.

Mathew Street Gallery, above The Beatles shop, Cavern Quarter, T0151-236 0009. See the Astrid Kirchherr and Klaus Voorman black and white portraits here alongside displays and exhibitions about the life and times of the Beatles.

Next to the Maritime Museum, the **Tate Liverpool** ① *The Colonnades, T0151-702 7400, www.tate.org.uk/liverpool, daily 1000-1730, free*, is the original Tate Modern, with four floors of modern art and regular exhibitions by major international artists including exhibitions touring from the London Tate Modern. There's something about it that doesn't work quite so well – the building has nothing of Bankside Power Station's buzz, and the low ceilings make it feel a little flat – it does host some interesting artist talks though.

Pier Head

From the Albert Dock you can take a walk along the Mersey on the **Riverside Walk** to Pier Head, another area of significant redevelopment. It only takes a few minutes and you'll walk past one of Liverpool's most famous buildings, the **Liver Insurance Building** (pronounced like 'driver' rather than 'river'). It was built in 1910 as one of the world's first multi-storey reinforced concrete buildings and its clock, 'The Great George', has the largest face of any of Britain's clocks. Before it was brought to Liverpool, one of the faces was used as a dinner table to seat 40 people. At the top of the building are the Liver Birds, one of the city's symbols. The mythical species of bird owe their creation to an ancient corporation seal of the town which originally featured an eagle. Over the centuries it began to look more like a cormorant until it became the figure it is today. Local legend says that if they fly away, the city will cease to exist.

Also here is one of the city's newest additions, the **Museum of Liverpool** ① *Pier Head, T0151-478 4545, www.liverpoolmuseums.org.uk, daily 1000-1700, free*, which opened in 2011. Housed in a futuristic landmark building right on the waterfront, the museum explores the story of Liverpool and how the city's port, its people and its history have shaped the city into one of global significance. With exhibits on everything from football (including a fascinating 15-minute film), poverty and the railroad to the Beatles and Brookside, a visit to Liverpool wouldn't be complete without it.

The **Open Eye Gallery** ⓘ *19 Mann Island, T0151-236 6768, www.openeye.org.uk, Tue-Sun 1030-1730, free*, was developed to exhibit photography, film and video and has survived being flooded, burnt out and prosecuted for obscenity to become one of the best photo and new media galleries in England.

Pier Head itself is the home of **Mersey Ferries** ⓘ *T0151-330 1444, www.mersey ferries.co.uk*. Too many people warble the old 'ferree cross the mersee' song for it really to be worth mentioning, but that's exactly what you can do from here on the 50-minute **Daily River Explorer Cruise** (£8 return, child £4.50 return, hourly departures). Liverpool grew up as a city around this port and the opportunities that it brought the people and the area have shaped it. It's the best way to see the city from the murky Mersey and takes you through 850 years of the city's history. The ferry also stops at the Seacombe Ferry Terminal in the Wirral (for Spaceport, see page 73) and the Woodside Ferry Terminal (for the U-Boat Story, see page 73); joint entry and ferry tickets available. A new attraction is the **Manchester Ship Canal Cruise** (six hours, £38, child £36), a 35-mile trip from Liverpool to Salford Quays along one of Britain's grandest canals.

Cavern Quarter

More like a tiny fraction than a quarter with its three small streets, this area has had a disproportionately huge impact on the city as a whole. It's the home of **The Cavern Club** where the Beatles first found fame, providing more photo opportunities than anywhere else in the city. You can slink your arm around a young bronze John Lennon on Mathew Street as he lounges against a wall covered in names. This wall of fame celebrates the bands who have rocked the Cavern since 1957 from the glass-shattering voice of Cilla Black to the more recent sneer of Oasis. The Cavern Club opposite is a dingy little bar and club that's still going strong. ▸▸ *See Live music, page 78*.

Nothing to do with the moptops is the intimate **View Two Gallery** ⓘ *23 Mathew St, T0151-236 9444, www.viewtwogallery.co.uk, Thu-Sat 1200-1600, free*, three floors of modern art in a townhouse. It's got wooden floorboards, white space and a particularly good gallery on the top floor, making it an oasis of calm amid the blatant tourism of the street below.

The end of Stanley Street leads on to Victoria Street with some upmarket bars and restaurants which are worth visiting later on in the evening. From Mathew Street you can also traverse **Cavern Walks** to the pedestrian precinct, a small indoor shopping centre with designer shops and a couple of cafés nestled around a bronze group of Beatles.

Walker Art Gallery

ⓘ *T0151-478 4199, www.walkerartgallery.org.uk, daily 1000-1700, free*.

Adjacent to Liverpool Lime Street station on William Brown Street stands the grand Walker Art Gallery. Unlike most of Liverpool's art galleries, the Walker has a varied collection of paintings and sculptures dating from before 1950, including masterpieces by Rembrandt and a selection of Impressionist paintings. There's only a small collection of modern art here, but that's pretty special too, with David Hockney hanging beside Gilbert and George. It's the city's biggest and most varied collection and one of the institutions that drove Liverpool's bid to be the European Capital of Culture in 2008.

Just around the corner is the **World Museum** ⓘ *William Brown St, T0151-478 4199, www.walkerartgallery.org.uk, daily 1000-1700, free,* where visitors can discover treasures from around the world, explore outer space and meet live creatures in the bug house, aquarium and planetarium. There are also exhibits on world cultures and the ancient world.

Around Hanover Street

From the outside, the Gostins Building on Hanover Street looks like so many of those around it – a dishevelled and ramshackle office block – but inside it's a treasure trove. The ground floor houses **The View Gallery** ⓘ *T0151-709 7273, Mon-Fri 1000-1700, Sat 1200-1600, Sun closed, free,* View Two's big brother and a former furniture showroom. It's a private art gallery with quirky pieces of furniture and contemporary paintings going back far into the building. The modern paintings, predominantly by professional artists from the Northwest, are very interesting, particularly the owner's own politically slanted photo-collages. It's got all the atmosphere that the Tate Liverpool is crying out for – and you're likely to get a personal tour and a glass of wine too.

Hope Street and the cathedrals

The Hope Street area, which leads up to the university village, houses two of Liverpool's landmarks. At one end, the Roman Catholic Metropolitan Cathedral (locals call it *Paddy's wigwam*) with its spiky crown and concrete façade looks down to the docks, and, at the other, the tower of the Anglican Cathedral provides an amazing view of the city. The **Metropolitan Cathedral** ⓘ *T0151-709 9222, www.liverpoolmetrocathedral.org.uk, 0730-1800, guides available, suggested donation £2.50,* is a distinctive building built 1962-1967 with an inspiring theatrical feel inside and Mondrian-inspired stained glass filtering the light down into the centre point.

The **Anglican Cathedral** ⓘ *T0151-709 6271, www.liverpoolcathedral.org.uk, Mon-Fri 0900-1700, guides available, suggested donation £3.50; cathedral tower and audio tour £5, concessions £4,* was described by Sir John Betjeman as "one of the great buildings of the world" and it's hard not to feel affected once you've stepped inside. The sheer volume of space inside is astounding. The cathedral's vaulted roof is so high that you feel swallowed up, and there's an option to go 331 ft up the tower for a view of the city. It's the largest Anglican cathedral in Europe, and the bells have the highest and heaviest peals in the world. The Foundation stone for the Anglican Cathedral was laid in 1904, but the Service of Dedication and Thanksgiving for Completion didn't happen until 1978. It's also a great place to eat with its **Mezzanine Café Bar** and **Welsford** restaurant.

Around Liverpool and Merseyside → *For listings, see pages 74-80.*

Saturdays bring another kind of pilgrimage to two other places of worship for Liverpudlians: Goodison and Anfield. The city's two football teams, Liverpool and Everton, have an interesting history. Everton used to play at Anfield, years ago before rent disputes caused them to move to another stadium, and Liverpool FC were created to play in the empty stadium they left behind.

The fans are rivals but, unusually, derby games see them standing in mixed supporters stands because they all get along. Over the years Liverpool has been responsible for nurturing many of England's most influential players including John Barnes, Steve

MacManaman, Michael Owen and Steven Gerrard, while Everton can claim responsibility for developing the early career of Wayne Rooney. You can visit the Kop and the bulging trophy cabinets at **Anfield** ① *Anfield Rd, 3 miles south of the centre, T0151-260 6677, www.liverpoolfc.com, museum daily 1000-1700, £5, child £3, for stadium tour see page 79.* Take a 17B, 17C, 17D or 217 bus from Queen Sq bus station.

Speke Hall ① *(NT), T0151-427 7231, Nov-Jul Wed-Sun 0900-1600, Jul-Sep Tue-Sun 1030-1700, house and gardens £9, child £4.50,* is a beautiful half-timbered Tudor mansion house dating from 1490, surrounded by a maze and some gorgeous woodland walks just eight miles to the south of the city centre. Actors dress up in Tudor gear for tours if you're after something atmospheric. Speke Hall is owned by the National Trust who more recently purchased another significant Liverpudlian property: **20 Forthlin Road** ① *(NT), Allerton, T0844-800 4791, www.nationaltrust.org.uk/beatles, Mar-Oct Wed-Sat, Nov-Dec Sat only, £20, child £5, admission by guided tour only,* the house where Paul McCartney grew up and where he and John Lennon used to practise riffs in the kitchen. It's the only original Beatles house that you can look around and can only be reached by minibus from Speke Hall or the Albert Dock.

The Wirral → *www.visitwirral.com.*

The Wirral Peninsula is situated between the River Dee and the River Mersey, overlooking both the Welsh Hills and the Liverpool skyline. It has a number of visitor attractions, some of which can be reached by ferry from Pier Head, as well as a Michelin-starred restaurant.

The **Port Sunlight Museum and Garden** ① *23 King George's Drive, just off Greendale Rd, Port Sunlight, T0151-644 6466, www.portsunlightvillage.com, daily 1000-1700, £3.75, concessions £3, child £2, self-guided walking trail £1,* is a picturesque 19th-century village just outside Bebington. It was originally created for the workers of Lever's soap factory by William Hesketh Lever. It's now a conservation area with landscaped gardens, primarily a tourist attraction as a 19th-century village stuck in time, all the more strange for being so close to the metropolis of Liverpool.

Set in a beautiful building a couple of roads down from Port Sunlight is the **Lady Lever Art Gallery** ① *Port Sunlight Village, T0151-478 4136, www.portsunlight.org.uk/gallery, Mon-Sat 1000-1700, Sun 1200-1700, free,* part of the Liverpool Museums collection. Founded by William Hesketh Lever (1851-1925), the museum is dedicated to the memory of his wife Elizabeth. The ground floor exhibition room displays one of the UK's finest collections of sculptures, paintings and decorative art including pottery, furniture and tapestries.

Near the Seacombe Ferry Terminal, **Spaceport** ① *Victoria Place, Seacombe, Wallasey, T0151-330 1566, www.spaceport.org.uk, Tue-Sun 1030-1800, £8, concessions £5.50, child £4.50; joint tickets available with Daily River Explorer Cruise (see page 71) and U-Boat Story,* is a £10 million attraction that takes you on a journey through space, as you walk through several themed galleries, which all feature a large variety of interactive hands-on exhibits and audiovisual experiences.

U-Boat Story ① *Woodside Ferry Terminal, Birkenhead, T0151-330 1000, www.u-boat story.co.uk, daily 1030-1730, £6, concessions £5, child £4; joint tickets available with Daily River Explorer Cruise (see page 71) and Spaceport, free guided tours at 1400,* is housed inside a real German U-boat and gives a unique insight into life on board a submarine during wartime. It's a fascinating look back in time, full of interactive and audiovisual displays, an original film archive and an exhibit on the enduring mystery of the *U-534.*

Liverpool listings

For hotel and restaurant price codes and other relevant information, see pages 9-12.

⬤ Where to stay

Liverpool *p64, map p68*
The Sefton Park area has a number of guesthouses and hotels 3 miles south of the city centre towards Speke. The tourist office can book beds for free around Merseyside.
£££ Hard Days Night Hotel, Central Buildings North John St, next to **The Cavern Club**, T0151-236 1964, www.harddays nighthotel.com. Upmarket Beatles-themed hotel in a historic building a 10-min walk from the Albert Dock. Rooms are modern and luxurious with 'Fab Four' artwork on the walls, flatscreen TV and Wi-Fi. Real fans should rent the John Lennon suite, complete with grand piano. There's also the innovative **Blakes** restaurant and **Bar Four** cocktail bar.
£££-££ Hope Street Hotel, 40 Hope St, T0151-709 3000, www.hopestreethotel.co.uk. Central 4-star hotel with fantastic views across the city. Rooms have chunky wooden furniture, solid wood floors and underfloor heating. The **London Carriage Works** restaurant is attached.
£££-££ Hotel Indigo Liverpool, 10 Chapel St, T0151-559 0111, www.hotelindigo liverpool.co.uk. Stylish hotel, more colourful than most, with Liverpuddlian-inspired decor and Marco Pierre White restaurant on site. Rooms have flatscreen TV and Wi-Fi.
£££-££ Base2Stay, 29 Seel St, T0151-705 2626, www.base2stay.com. Modern furnished rooms to rent with kitchenette and Wi-Fi.
££ Blenheim Lakeside Hotel, 37 Aigburth Dr, T0151-727 7380, www.blenheimlake sidehotel.co.uk. A private guesthouse that was once the house of Stu Sutcliffe, the Beatle who never was.
££ Heywood House Hotel, 11 Fenwick St, T0151-224 1444, www.heywoodhouse

hotel.co.uk. Describing itself as a 'budetique hotel', the good-value rooms range from 'comfy' to 'plush'. The hotel itself has quirky architectural design features throughout.
££ Malmaison Liverpool, Princes Dock, 7 William Jessop Way, T0151-229 5000, www.malmaison.com. Located near the Liver building and overlooking the Mersey, rooms have contemporary design and all mod cons.
££ Regent Maritime Hotel, 56-68 Regent Rd, Bootle, T0151-922 4090, www.regent maritimehotel.com. About 2 miles away on the dock from Pier Head in Bootle. It's a very reasonable B&B with some large split-level bedrooms and a bar and restaurant.
££-£ Aachen Hotel, 89-91 Mount Pleasant, T0151-709 3633, www.aachenhotel.co.uk. A small, central and friendly place with fairly basic rooms and all-you-can-eat breakfast.
£ Embassie Hostel, 1 Falkner Sq, Toxteth, out of town to the south past Chinatown, T0151-707 1089, www.embassie.com. A bit out of town but one of the cheapest place to stay in Liverpool in a Georgian townhouse with relaxed and friendly atmosphere. Lots of freebies to entice people away from the centre, including internet, free Beatles tour on Thu, free parking, free breakfast, tea and coffee.
£ International Inn, 4 South Hunter St off Hardman St (just off Hope St), T0151-709 8135, www.internationalinn.co.uk. Set in a Victorian warehouse this friendly hostel is centrally located and very modern in design. From hostel dorms to superior hotel-style rooms or self-catering apartments. Free Wi-Fi, tea, coffee and toast. Also runs the **Cocoon Pod Hotel**, www.cocoonliverpool.co.uk, for those looking for something a bit different.
£ Liverpool YHA, 25 Tabley St, off Wapping, T0845-371 9527, www.yha.org.uk/ hostel/liverpool. Very close to Albert Dock this is a big purpose-built hostel with a restaurant, laundry, games room.

Liverpool p64, map p68

Liverpool has food from Asia and Europe right through to traditional hotpot and cheap hangover brunches for that Sunday morning feeling. Many of the bars are cafés during the day and you'll always find a trendy corner in the Ropewalks to watch the beautiful people if that's what you're after. Chinatown's Nelson St is lined with Chinese restaurants, and the Albert Dock caters for tourists during the day with cheap cafés and for the more selective crowd in its underground industrial vaults in the evening. The most fashionable and new restaurants are clustered around Victoria St, with their minimalist interiors and soft leather armchairs, and Hope St just off the Ropewalks has some exclusive places to eat too.

£££ Panoramic 34, West Tower, 34th floor, 10 Brook St, T0151-236 5534, www.panoramicliverpool.com. Dine 300 ft above the city in one of the UK's highest restaurants. It's a fairly spectacular view and the food is simple and classic.

£££-££ London Carriage Works, Hope Street Hotel, 40 Hope St, T0151-709 3000, www.thelondoncarriageworks.co.uk. Focuses on fresh local ingredients with charcuterie platters to share and tempting mains including loin of Lakeland rabbit or Wirral pork cooked 3 ways.

£££-££ Puschka, 16 Rodney St, T0151-708 8698, www.puschka.co.uk. Funky little European place with a reputation for good food and good service. The menu includes tempting beetroot-cured salmon, chicken liver and cognac parfait and slow braised venison daube, as well as plenty of vegetarian options. It's just down the hill from Hope St towards the Ropeworks. Quirky bohemian atmosphere.

££ 60 Hope Street, T0151-707 6060, www.60hopestreet.com. Towards the Anglican cathedral is a modern restaurant in a Georgian townhouse. It serves pancetta-wrapped kidneys and grilled sea bass upstairs and has a cheaper bistro in the same style with steak and chips and good chocolate brownies downstairs. Fairly exclusive but not snooty. Closed Sun.

££ Blue Bar and Grill, 17 Edward Pavilion, Albert Dock, T0151-702 5831. Daily 1100-0300. A basement bar-club with a relaxed lounge atmosphere serving tapas and Portuguese food. It's known as a footballer hang-out and is your best bet for spotting Liverpool FC's superstar players.

££ Café Tabac, 126 Bold St, T0151-709 9502, www.cafetabac.co.uk. One of the city's trendy options with home-made soup and reasonably priced Sunday roasts with a twist just at the bottom of this price category.

££ Eureka, 7 Myrtle Pde, T0151-709 7225, www.eurekarestaurantliverpool.co.uk. A really popular place with the locals, it's a Greek restaurant that's cheap, cheerful and complete with chirpy Greek pop soundtrack.

££ Gusto, Unit 6, Edward Pavillion, Albert Dock, T0151-708 6969, www.gustorest aurants.uk.com/restaurants/gusto-liverpool. Have dinner here and there'll be enough money left over to move to the **Blue Bar** for celeb-spotting.

££ Hanover Street Social, Casartelli Building, 16-20 Hanover St, T0151-709 8784, www.hanoverstreetsocial.co.uk. Lively modern brasserie with industrial features such as exposed bricks, air ducts and a metal cocktail bar. All-day menu includes comforting rustic dishes such as grilled goat's cheese on brioche with fig and blueberry jam, crisp pork belly with Stonaway black pudding.

££-£ Lunya, 18-20 College Lane, T0151-706 9770, www.lunya.co.uk. Restaurant and deli with a huge Spanish and Catalan menu. Tapas, plates to share or tasting banquets.

£ Hannah's, 2 Leece St, T0151-708 5959, www.barhannah.co.uk. Simple fare such as paninis and speciality burgers eaten in the glass roof terrace with spectacular views.
£ HOST, 31 Hope St, T0151-708 5831, www.ho-st.co.uk. Pan-Asian restaurant offering Thai, Chinese and Japanese food in simple surrounds. Has a whole range of dishes to cater for dietary requirements such as vegan, gluten- and dairy-free.
£ The Quarter, 10 Falkner St, T0151-707 1965, www.thequarteruk.com. Italian-inspired restaurant and deli with more than just pizza and pasta. Great tasting cheap eats.

Cafés
Art Café, 483 West Derby Rd, Tuebrook, overlooking Newsham Park in the north of the city, T0151-263 9463, www.liverpool artcafe.co.uk. This amazingly cheap café exhibits local and recent Liverpool graduates contemporary artwork and does a good line in herbal teas and cheap muffins.
Egg Café, 16 Newington, close to Liverpool Central train station, T0151-707 2755, www.eggcafe.co.uk. In the loft of an old Victorian building, this vegetarian café offers panoramic views and an arty bohemian feel.
LEAF, 65-67 Bold St, T0151-707 7747, www.thisisleaf.co.uk. Tea shop and café that's a hub for local creative talent as well as serving wholesome food and several varieties of loose leaf tea. Events include open mic nights and live music,

---

Around Liverpool and Merseyside *p72*
£££ Restaurant Fraiche, 11 Rose Mount, Oxton, T0151-652 2914, www.restaurant fraiche.com. Michelin-star restaurant serving modern cuisine in a sophisticated but simple setting. Signature dishes include wild brill fillet with parsley quinoa, grape and rose or loin of venison with pickled grellot and kohlrabi. There's also a 6-course tasting menu with complementary wine selection. Immaculate service and presentation.

Pubs, bars and clubs

Liverpool *p64, map p68*
Liverpudlians are proud of their nightlife. Concentrated in a small area you can find everything you could want from cosy pubs to sophisticated bars and trend-setting clubs that stay open until 0700. **Bold St** was the original rope walk, the area providing the rope for the city's shipping trade. **Ropewalks** is now a cosmopolitan strip, nothing remotely ropey about it, and the streets are jumping on Fri and Sat nights. If in doubt, head down to **Concert Square**, which is always buzzing on a weekend, and follow the crowd.

Pubs and bars
Alma de Cuba, St Peter's Church, Seel St, T0151-702 7394, www.alma-de-cuba.com. Once a Polish church, now a flamboyant Cuban bar and restaurant with Latin American cocktail menu. Always packed at the weekend, expect a queue to get in.
Attic Bar, 33-45 Parr St, T0151-708 6345, www.theatticliverpool.com. Tucked away down a back street but worth seeking out for its intimate atmosphere and huge selection of world beers. The signature cocktails and burger bar are an added bonus.
Baa Bar, 7 Myrtle St, T0151-707 0610, www.baabar.co.uk, Liverpool's original trendy bar with some bargain drink offers and 2 floors of dancey, funky music. Hosts the Rawhide comedy night every Tue.
The Cavern Club, 10 Mathew St, T0151-236 9091, www.cavernclub.org. Has live music most nights (see Live music, below). You'll also find a host of basement bars here, many with Beatles pictures on the walls or some other tacky connection. You won't hear much Scouse spoken in this area as these bars cater overwhelmingly for tourists.
Circo, Britannia House, Albert Dock, T0151-709 0470, www.circoliverpool.com. Trendy 2-floor bar, restaurant and cocktail lounge

that transforms into one of the busiest spots in Liverpool at weekends playing a mixture of soul, funk, disco and house music. Also has 'freak shows' such as fire eaters.

Fly in the Loaf, 13 Hardman St, T0151-708 0817, www.flyintheloaf.co.uk. Traditional English pub, particularly popular during sporting events and Oktoberfest, with 60 world beers and 6 cask ales.

G-bar, 1-7 Eberle St, T0151-236 4416, www.g-bar.com. Has a kitschy crowd: gay, straight and everything in between, all dressed up to the nines.

Korova, 39-41 Fleet St, T0151-709 7097, www.korova-liverpool.com. Cool alternative bar with an eclectic line-up of live music. Attracts a less mainstream crowd.

Modo, 2 Concert Sq, T0151-709 8832, www.modoliverpool.co.uk. Attracts a mixture of young professionals and students. Cocktail bar and club.

PanAm Bar, 22 Britannia Pavilion, Albert Dock, T0151-702 5831, www.panambar liverpool.co.uk. Has (Scouse accents notwithstanding) a real New York atmosphere. It's a fashionable place in a warehouse conversion with stone floor, dimly lit booths and steak-style food.

Philharmonic Dining Rooms, 36 Hope St, T0151-707 2837. It was built in 1900 in imitation of the gentlemen's club. There are a lot of pubs in Liverpool, but nowhere else will you find William Morris wallpaper, Art Nouveau tiling and marble urinals.

Revolution, 18 Wood St, T0151-707 1933. Also has venues at Albert Dock; in the Cavern Quarter at 2 Temple Court; and in the Tea Factory Building on St Peter's Square. Serves vodka in a million different flavours and has a decent cocktail menu for saints or sinners.

Thomas Rigby's, 23-25 Dale St, T0151-236 3269. A Grade II-listed former coaching house now a friendly pub with a large selection of global beers. Looks a bit run-down from the outside but inside it's cosy with a large bar and plenty of atmosphere.

Ye Cracke, 13 Rice St, T0151-709 4171. 19th-century pub frequented by John Lennon in his art school days. It's a very cheap pub with cozy snugs and value greasy-spoon meals.

Clubs

Cream, www.cream.co.uk. Based in the **Nation** nightclub, a massive dance music venue with 3 rooms and a 1400 capacity. The legendary weekly house nights that produced many spin-offs, including a record label, stopped in 2002, having played host to top DJs including Paul Oakenfold (who was resident DJ 1997-1999), Paul van Dyk, Sasha plus early exclusive DJ sets from The Chemical Brothers. It still holds sell-out events about 4 times a year (Easter, May Bank Holiday, Oct/Nov and Boxing night). If you're a serious clubber, no doubt you've already been to one of Cream's paler imitations somewhere around the country. Be sure to book well ahead.

Garlands, Carlton Hall, 8-10 Eberle St, T0151-2311105, www.garlandsonline.com. It's a riot of colour and attitude, a mixed gay and straight crowd dressed flamboyantly and out for a good time. It's an antidote to big warehouse clubs, broken down into smaller rooms, and the sort of place you expect to see a drag queen or 2. Sat is the night to go.

Heebie Jeebies, 80-82 Seal St, T0151-709 3678. 3 floors of dancing with uber-cool decor, tunnels of brick and an underground feel. Classic indie and regular rock nights. Live bands play on the courtyard in summer.

The Magnet, 45 Hardman St, T0151-709 4000, http://themagnetliverpool.com. Club and live music venue 5 mins' from Lime St station. Has some of the best alternative RnB club nights, house music events, rock n roll sounds and DnB. After parties go on very late.

Zanzibar Club, 43 Seel St, T0151-707 0633, www.thezanzibarclub.com. Small live music venue with good acoustics known for its regular club nights including The Bandwagon and Valhalla. There's a chill-out room with cushions to crash out on upstairs.

Liverpool p64, map p68
Cinema and theatre
Everyman Theatre, 5-9 Hope St, T0151-709 4776, www.everymanplayhouse.com. A top venue for anything from small touring productions, classic theatre and Shakespeare to new plays, poetry and comedy.

Foundation for Art and Creative Technology (**FACT**), Wood St, T0151-707 4464, www.fact.co.uk. One of the UK's leading media centres for the support and development of film, video and new media projects, it is painfully cutting edge. Inside the complex there's an independent cinema, The Picturehouse, galleries, internet and a bar.

Liverpool Playhouse, Williamson Sq, T0151-709 4776, www.everymanplay house.com. This is a more grown-up theatre, at the Shakespeare end and not so experimental but attracting big name actors and touring productions.

Unity Theatre, 1 Hope Pl, T0844-873 2888, www.unitytheatreliverpool.co.uk. An intimate space with a varied programme of dance, music and film.

Comedy clubs
From the city that gave the world Ken Dodd, Liverpool's comedy scene is surprisingly not bad at all.

Comedy Central, The Vaults, 17 Edwardian Pavillion, Albert Dock, T0151-702 5831, www.jicomedy.co.uk. In the plush Baby Blue bar, with meal deal available, attracts some big names.

Envi, 17-21 Fleet St, T0151-709 3498, www.enviliverpool.com. When the dance floor isn't packed with party-goers it hosts some decent comedy nights.

Rawhide Comedy Club, in the downstairs bar at Royal Court Liverpool Theatre (see below), T0870-7871866, www.rawhide comedy.com. Hosts TV comedians and international rib ticklers.

Royal Court Theatre, 1 Roe St, T0151-709 4321, www.royalcourtliverpool.co.uk. Touring stand-ups and a variety of acts.

Live music
Academy, Blundell Street, 63-65 Blundell St, Albert Dock, T0151-7095779, www.blundellstreetliverpool.com. A kind of lounge bar/easy listening music venue with an authentic 50s vibe, skilfully circumventing the kitsch image of the genre with small candlelit booths and a classy atmosphere. There are live acts here most nights for you to listen to while sipping cocktails, and they serve food too.

Bluecoat, School Lane, T0151-707 5297, www.thebluecoat.org.uk. The oldest Grade I-listed building in Liverpool and recently refurbished to create a space for creative arts such as music, literature and dance. It's a hub for new talent and the creative community.

The Cavern Club, Mathew St, T0151-222 1957, www.cavernclub.org. Has live music most days of varying quality with a stone floor and a slightly grotty feel. There's a lot of wannabees here and it doesn't really live up to its image as the first step on the ladder to fame.

Echo Arena, Kings Dock, ACC Liverpool complex, waterfront, T0151-475 8888, www.echoarena.com. Opened in 2008 for the launch event of the European Capital of Culture. The stadium has a capacity of 10,000 people and is where all the big names play when they come to town including Shirley Bassey, Elton John, Beyonce and Bob Dylan.

Picket Warehouse, 61 Jordan St, T0151-708 6789, www.myspace.com/picketliverpool. Liverpool's favourite live music venue where you're most likely to catch the next big thing. They have a wide range of performers from the latest chart sensations to young breakthrough indie bands and Peruvian banjo players.

The Royal Liverpool Philharmonic, Liverpool Philharmonic Hall, 36 Hope St,

T0151-709 3789, www.liverpoolphil.com.
Home to the city's orchestra, the Phil, the hall has a regular programme of classical music and a Schumann festival in Jan and Feb each year. If you want to hear classical music, this is the best place, and it's a quirky hall with its art deco design and also shows classic films, music and comedy.

✪ Festivals

Liverpool *p64, map p68*
Aug Creamfields, T0151-709 1693, www.creamfields.com. The dance music festival hosted by Cream every year on the Aug Bank Holiday weekend, regularly voted the best dance event in the UK. Tickets cost around £120 and sell out fast.
Aug International Beatle Week, run by the Cavern Club at the end of August, www.cavernclub.org/beatleweek. This is the biggest celebration of Beatles music in the world, with numerous sound- and look-alike bands in venues throughout the city. It incorporates the **Mathew St Festival**, a free music festival with over 200 bands.

◯ Shopping

Liverpool *p64, map p68*
Shopping in Liverpool is not as varied or interesting as Leeds or Manchester but the new **Liverpool ONE** centre has filled a much-needed gap, and there are a few little places, particularly along **Bold St**, where you can find something unique, rather than more Beatles memorabilia.
3 Beat Records, 5 Slater St, T0151-709 3355, www.3brecords.co.uk. Independent music store and ticket outlet specializing in vinyl, CDs, tickets and DJ equipment.
The Beatles Shop, 31 Mathew St, T0151-236 8066, www.thebeatleshop.co.uk. Has the largest selection of Beatles stuff in the world alongside rare records and a jukebox.

Bluecoat, School Lane, just off the Ropewalks, T0151-707 5297. Arts centre, good for picking up contemporary crafts and design.
Cavern Walks Shopping Centre, Mathew St, T0151-236 9082, www.cavern-walks.co.uk. Has a number of small clothes shops selling designer and clubby gear.
Liverpool ONE, 5 Wall St, T0151-232 3100, www.liverpool-one.com. Opened in 2008 on the site of 42 acres of disused land in the city centre, this is the city's smart new shopping, residential and leisure complex with top designers as well as high street brands. You'll find pretty much everything here from ultra-hip fashion brands to Liverpool and Everton football strips.
Utility, 86 Bold St, T0151-707 9919, www.utilitydesign.co.uk; also in **Liverpool ONE**. Boutique gift and homeware shop with an eclectic mix of contemporary crafts, homeware and fashion.

⛰ What to do

Liverpool *p64, map p68*
Football
You're very unlikely to be able to get tickets for either of Liverpool's premiership sides, but you can visit both stadiums and check out the trophies, stadia and see behind the scenes. Turn up at Goodison Park for Everton on a match day and you might be lucky.
Anfield Stadium and Museum Tour, T05601-595800, www.anfieldtour.com. Go behind the scenes at one of football's most famous stadiums, £8.50 includes museum, concessions £5.50. The **Anfield Experience** is a full-day at the stadium including lunch and the chance to meet Liverpool legends.
Goodison Park Tour, T0151-530 5212, www.evertonfc.com. Stadium Tour Experience £10, child £5, Mon, Wed, Fri and Sun at 1100 and 1300 except on match days.

Horse racing

Aintree Racecourse, Ormskirk Rd, Aintree, T0151-5232600, www.aintree.co.uk, a 15-min train ride from the city centre. Famous for hosting the Grand National every year on the second Sat in Apr. If you're into racing but in Liverpool at the wrong time, the racecourse has a Grand National simulator and racecourse tours, including the Grand National Experience.

Tours

The **City Explorer** bus offers hop-on hop-off bus tours of the city to all the main sights with a commentary. It's a good way to see the city if short on time.

Magical Mystery Tours, run by Cavern City Tours, T0151-236 9091, www.cavernclub.org/the-magical-mystery-tour. 2-hr trips in vintage buses showing where the Fab Four grew up, with landmarks including John Lennon's childhood home on Penny Lane and Strawberry Fields, before finishing at the Cavern. Tours leave from outside the tourist information centre at Albert Dock, daily at 1130 and 1400, tickets £15.95.

Mersey Tunnel Tour, leaves from George's Dock Building, George's Dock, Pier Head, T0151-330 4504, www.merseytravel.gov.uk, Tue, Wed, Thu (1700) and Sat (1000), book in advance, £5, no children under the age of 10. Tour of the Queensway Tunnel that takes you behind the scenes to visit the control room, learn about the construction of the tunnel and admire the engineering that changed the history of Liverpool.

Yellow Duckmarine Tour, tickets from Anchor Courtyard, T0151-708 7799, www.theyellowduckmarine.co.uk. Odd yellow vehicles taking you from Atlantic Pavilion in the Albert Dock around the city's waterfront, city and dock areas. It's not the yellow submarine, but it's not far off. Tickets cost £15.95, concessions £9.95, child £10.95, for which you get a 1-hr land and sea tour. Tours depart from Gower St bus stop, Albert Dock, every 30 mins from 1030.

⊖ Transport

Liverpool *p64, map p68*
Bus
National Express, T08705-808080, www.nationalexpress.co.uk, has regular services to major towns and cities in Britain from the Norton St Coach Station. **London Victoria** 12 times daily (5 hrs), **Birmingham** 12 times daily (3 hrs), **Manchester** hourly (1 ½ hrs), **Blackpool** 8 times daily (1 hr 45 mins), **Newcastle** 3 times daily (6½ hrs), **Edinburgh** 7 times daily (8 hrs).

Car
Avis, 113 Mulberry St, T0151-709 4737; **Easycar**, NCP car park Paradise St, www.easycar.com; **Skydrive UK**, South Terminal Lennon Airport, T0151-448 0000.

Taxis
Mersey Cabs, T0151-298 2222, T0151-207 2222, www.merseycabs.co.uk or the ranks up by Lime St station, on Whitechapel or Clayton Sq.

Train
From Liverpool Lime St you can reach most major UK destinations, including **Manchester**, (1 hr), **Birmingham** (1½ hrs), **Chester** (40 mins) and **London Euston**, (3-4 hrs), on **Virgin** trains, www.virgin trains.com. Contact www.thetrainline.com for the cheapest tickets.

Lancashire

Lancashire is a diverse mix of the constituent parts of the North of England. To the north, the county borders Cumbria with stunning views, lakes, mountains and moors; in the south, Manchester spreads into the dark mill towns of Preston, Blackburn and Burnley. The county town of Lancaster in the northwest is historic and beautiful with wide cobbled streets and country pubs. The working castle in the town is the final destination of the Pendle Witch Tour, tracing the steps of 10 witches from the eastern part of the county who were condemned to hang during the 17th century. This eastern part of the country borders Yorkshire where the Lancashire forests meet the dales.

Lancashire in general is not well-visited by tourists. The southernmost towns are not geared up for mass tourism, but the northern and eastern countryside is great walking country, and you'll receive a warm Lancastrian welcome in the small stone villages. There is, however, one spot in the county that gets more than its fair share of attention: the Las Vegas of the North, Blackpool. It's a traditional seaside resort that has got out of hand, with the largest rollercoaster in Europe and a Golden Mile of arcades and flashing lights. If Elvis had ever performed in England, it's unlikely that he would have held court in the ballroom here amid the kiss-me-quick hats, but then there are more than enough Elvis impersonators on each of the three piers to make up for that.

Arriving in Lancashire

Getting around The best and easiest way of exploring the region, particularly the charming country villages, is by car. Local buses run in Lancashire but are not always as frequent or regular as necessary. Train services between major towns in Lancashire, however, are very regular every day except Sunday and coach connections from Liverpool and Manchester to Blackpool are reliable, going every hour or more frequently. Manchester and Liverpool are the main coach, bus and air transport hubs in the Northwest, including Lancashire. ▸▸ *See Transport, page 93.*

Blackpool → *For listings, see pages 90-93.*

In reality, Blackpool is better described as the Bognor Regis of the North than the Vegas of the North. The town has got the biggest glitterball in the world, weighing 4.5 tonnes and a host of claims to fame including the Pleasure Beach, a huge park with amusement arcades and rollercoasters. The Blackpool Illuminations run from the end of August to early November, a swathe of neon lights along the promenade overlooking the seven miles of yellow sand, lighting up the many chip shops, gypsy fortune tellers and candy floss stalls along the Golden Mile. Tacky, bold, brash and particularly crowded on a hot summer bank holiday Monday, Blackpool can give you a good time if you like rollercoasters and don't mind paying over the odds for the tourist attractions.

As with many other Northern towns, money has been ploughed into the town in the last 10 years and a large regeneration project has been underway. Waterloo Road in South Shore has been transformed into a modern shopping centre and a £285 million project is planned to regenerate the rundown area north of the station into a world-class civic development and gateway to the city. The tower itself has even had a facelift. Blackpool might not be everyone's cup of tea, but it's hard not to have a good time here, and the town is striving to retain its place as Britain's top seaside resort.

Arriving in Blackpool

Getting there The station is walking distance from the centre of town on Talbot Road and has links with Scotland on **Virgin Trains** ① *T08457-222333, www.virgin.com/trains*, with the northeast of England on the **Transpennine Express**, and with Preston and Manchester with **First North Western** trains. Blackpool is easily reached by car from Manchester on the M61, M6 and M55, Leeds on the M62, M6 and M55 and the rest of Lancashire on the M6 and M55. **National Express** ① *T08705-808080, www.national express.co.uk*, runs regular coach services from Manchester and Liverpool. The coach stop is on Lonsdale Road in summer and Talbot Road during the winter season.

Tourist information Blackpool TIC ① *1 Clifton St near the North Pier, T01253-478222, www.visitblackpool.com, Mon-Fri 0900-1700; also at Festival House, on the promenade between North and Central Piers, Mon-Fri 0915-1700, Sun 1015-1530*, can book accommodation and sells discount tickets. The **Blackpool Resort Pass**, www.blackpoolresortpass.com, costs £52.50 for six attractions and £79 for nine attractions, and is well worth it if you're planning to visit the main sights. The websites www.blackpool.gov.uk and www.blackpooltourism.co.uk also have some useful visitor information.

Safety Blackpool is perennially busy with groups of young people thronging the promenade. Pickpockets are a problem in the town, particularly in the summer, and you should ensure that parked cars are locked with no valuables on display as break-ins are frequent. The beach is popular in the summer too and you should always take care in the water with regard to tides. In a coastal emergency call 999 and ask for the coastguard.

Places in Blackpool

You cannot consider yourself a true English seaside town unless you've got at least one pier. Blackpool, true to form, has gone over the top and has three. When they were first built in the 19th century there were only two, the **North Pier** and the **South Pier**, now there is also the **Central Pier**. The North was considered more prestigious and the working classes generally frequented the South. There isn't much to pick between them all now, except that you have to pay a small fee to visit the North Pier, which has a short

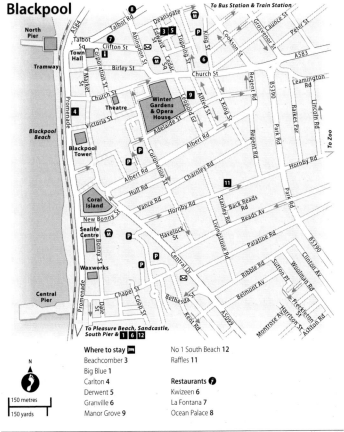

Blackpool

Where to stay 🛏
Beachcomber **3**
Big Blue **1**
Carlton **4**
Derwent **5**
Granville **6**
Manor Grove **9**

No 1 South Beach **12**
Raffles **11**

Restaurants 🍴
Kwizeen **6**
La Fontana **7**
Ocean Palace **8**

tram ride on it to take you to the end. All three piers are garish and have more arcades and stalls than is strictly necessary; the Central Pier also has a ferris wheel and other rides amid the Blackpool rock stalls. Alongside the Promenade it is possible to take pony and trap rides along the **Golden Mile**. Unlike other tourist resorts that view the end of August as the end of the season, Blackpool takes it as a cue to begin enticing visitors back to the town. The Illuminations, famed in 1879 for being like "artificial sunshine" and now for being an immense gaudy display of neon and plastic, are switched on at the end of August and carry on until the beginning of November.

The 518-ft **Blackpool Tower** ① *The Promenade, T01253-622242, www.theblackpool tower.co.uk, Mon-Fri 1000-1535, Sat-Sun 1000-1635, free entry includes access to the Intergalactic Games Zone, terrace views and ballroom balconies, prices for Tower, Ballroom and Jungle Jim's listed below, combined tickets available,* which first opened in 1894, was inspired by the Eiffel Tower and has long been the town's dominant landmark. It was given a makeover in 2011 and now features the **Blackpool Tower Eye** ① *£12.60, £9.60,* which starts with a 4D cinema experience before whizzing you up to the top in a lift to the glass SkyWalk for uninterrupted views of the sand and grey sea. Back down at the bottom there's the family-orientated **Tower Circus** ① *Apr-Nov, £12.60, child (3-13 years) £9.60, toddlers £1.40,* and the famous **Tower Ballroom** ① *free viewing from balconies, £9 to enter ballroom, children free,* with its spectacular dance floor. However, you might have a job to drag your kids away from **Jungle Jim's** ① *child (age 3-13) £6, toddler (age 0-3) £3, 1 adult free with every child,* an indoor adventure playground with a 'Lost City' theme. For the older ones, the **Blackpool Tower Dungeons** ① *Bank Hey St, T01253-622242, www.the-dungeons.co.uk/ blackpool/en, Mon-Fri 1100-1700, Sat-Sun 1000-1700, £15, discounts available online,* is a gory history-based attraction that recounts Blackpool's most gruesome tales, with a labyrinth of mirrors, drop ride and torture chamber amongst other spooky features.

Behind the tower, **St John's** is another new development area with trees, dancing fountains and the new *Wave* sculpture. The street hosts a variety of events and entertainment throughout the year. The **Winter Gardens** ① *97 Church St, T01253-625252, www.wintergardensblackpool.co.uk, daily 1100-1600,* houses the Opera House (one of the largest theatres in Europe) and the Pavillion Theatre and attracts some big names.

Heading south along The Promenade, just opposite Central Pier, the **Sea Life Centre** ① *T01253-751647, www.visitsealife.com/blackpool, £10, child £7,* has more than 200 creatures including sharks, octopus, seahorses and rays, as well as an interactive rockpool where you can hold a crab, touch a starfish or have a shrimp manicure. Just next door, **Madame Tussaud's** ① *T0871-282 9200, www.madametussauds.com/blackpool, daily 1000-1600, £15, child (age 3-15) £12,* offers five floors of waxworks that take you on a journey through the world of TV, music, film, sport and comedy.

At the other end of the Promenade, the **Pleasure Beach** ① *Ocean Blvd, T0870-444558, www.blackpoolpleasurebeach.co.uk, weekends only mid-Feb to Mar, Apr-Nov Sun-Fri 1000-1800, Sat 1000-2000 with longer hours in school holidays, Pleasure Beach Pass £6, wristband for rides £20,* is the real attraction in Blackpool with huge rollercoasters overlooking the sea and the southernmost end of the town. The **Big One** is Europe's tallest and fastest rollercoaster at 235 ft high and 87 mph, a massive structure that is closed on windy days. There are lots of other white-knuckle rides as well as arcades, candy floss stalls, cafés and tacky musical shows. Also here is **Nickelodeon Land** ① *child (over 12) £35, child (2-11) £30, 50% discount online,* featuring 12 rides and a whole host of Nickelodeon characters.

Also geared towards families, the **Sandcastle Waterpark** ① *South Promenade, T01253-343602, www.blackpool-sandcastle.co.uk, daily 0900-1800 in summer with varied seasonal opening hours, child (over 12 years) £12.50, child (3-11 years) £10.50*, is a huge swimming pool complex with 18 twisting wild water rides, chutes, saunas and sun loungers. Altogether much healthier than paddling or swimming in the sea.

A couple of miles from the seafront, the **Blackpool Zoo** ① *East Park Dr, T01253-830830, www.blackpoolzoo.org.uk, daily 1000-1630, £15.50, child (age 3-15) £11, free bus 21 from outside the Tower*, was recently voted one of the UK's top five zoos. There are more than 400 animals in captivity here including dolphins, mountain gorillas, orang-utans and elephants. It's fairly spacious as British zoos go.

Nearby, in Stanley Park, the **Blackpool Model Village** ① *East Park Drive, T01253-763827, www.blackpoolmodelvillage.com, Mar-Oct daily 1000-1600, Nov-Mar weekends only, £6.95, child (age 3-16) £5.75*, set in 2.5 acres of landscaped gardens, has hundreds of handcrafted models depicting British life in miniature, from a Cornish fishing village to a Scottish castle.

Lancaster → *For listings, see pages 90-93.*

Lancaster is the historic county town of Lancashire and was recently granted city status. The main feature of the town is its Norman castle, which until recently was used as a prison. It has held some notorious inmates in its time including the Pendle witches (see box, page 87) and the Birmingham Six. The town centre is compact and charming with wide cobbled streets and cosy traditional pubs. Just south of the Cumbrian border, it's a pleasant place to stop on the way to or from the Lakes.

Arriving in Lancaster
Getting there Lancaster is on the main West Coast railway line and on the Cumbrian coast line, with connections from Carlisle (one hour), Manchester (45 minutes) and Preston (25 minutes). There are bus services from Preston, Blackpool and the Lake District.

Tourist information Lancaster TIC ① *Storey Creative Industries Centre, Meeting House Lane T01524-582394, www.visitlancashire.com, daily 1000-1700*. The TIC can book accommodation and has information on walks around the city including Halloween and torchlit Old Calendar walks. **Catwalks of Lancaster** ① *T01524-792089, www.catwalks-lancaster.co.uk, Jul-Sep Thu 1930, £4, child £1*, runs a summer programme of guided themed walks, which leave from the castle gates and tell of ghosts and murderers, pubs, the Pendle witch trail and the town's history. The website www.citycoastcountryside.co.uk is also a useful source of information.

Places in Lancaster
Lancaster Castle ① *Castle Hill, T01524-64998, www.lancastercastle.com, daily 1000-1700, guided tours leave half hourly 1030-1600 from Shire Hall, no photography permitted, £5, concessions £4*, is the dominant building in Lancaster and has been since it was built in 1093. The castle is still used as a Crown Court and until March 2011 was also a Category C prison. The area used as a prison is not open to the public but it's possible to visit a good part of it and learn about its history on a guided tour. The hour-long trail takes visitors around the courts, the oldest parts of the castle, the old cells and hanging

corner and is well worth taking. The hill on which the castle stands was used as a fort by the Romans around AD 79, and in 1093 a Norman baron, Roger of Poitou, built a motte and bailey castle here. Fifty years later that was replaced by a stone keep, some of which survives today.

Adjacent to the castle, **Lancaster Priory** ① *Lancaster Priory, Castle Hill, T01524-582394, www.lancasterpriory.org, daily 1000-1630*, was built as a Benedictine priory in 1094. It is now a parish church and contains carved stones and crosses from the ninth to 11th centuries. There is a refectory inside the church serving teas and coffees. To the rear of the church on the hill are the remains of the old Roman baths.

In the centre of town and originally home to one of the witch hunters, Thomas Covell, the **Judges' Lodgings** ① *Castle Hill, T01524-32808, Mon-Fri 1300-1600, Sat-Sun 1000-1600, free*, is a beautiful Grade I-listed Georgian building. It has also been home to the chief jailor and afterwards became the residence of judges visiting the Assize courts. Inside the house is the **Town House Museum** and the **Museum of Childhood**, with dolls, toys and games from the 18th century, a large collection of Lancaster's delicate Gillow furniture and a portrait collection depicting the town's connections with the slave trade.

In the former customs house of Lancaster, the **Lancaster Maritime Museum** ① *Custom House, St George's Quay, T01524-64637, Apr-Oct daily 1100-1700, Nov-Mar daily 1230-1600, £3, children free*, explores the history of Lancaster as a port, the Lancaster canal, fishing and nearby Morecambe Bay. The exhibitions are brought alive with audiovisual stimuli, smells, sounds and reconstructions and provide an interesting history of the city's development.

Outside Lancaster

Overlooking the city to the south, the commanding Ashton Memorial folly in **Williamson Park** ① *off Wyresdale Rd, signposted from junctions 33 and 34 of the M6, T01524-33318, Oct-Mar daily 1000-1600, Apr-Sep 1000-1700, with theatre and special events throughout the year, free*, is visible from some distance. The ornate Victorian dome was commissioned by Lord Ashton, who made his fortune producing oilcloth and linoleum, as a tribute to his late wife. The 54-acre park itself is full of woodland walkways, terraced paths, water fountains and the **Butterfly House** ① *£3.60, child £2.60, guided tours Sat-Sun 1100*, which is designed to resemble a rainforest complete with trees, vines, foliage and colourful butterflies.

To the north of Lancaster on the M6 and A6, **Carnforth Station** ① *Warton Rd, Carnforth, T01524-735165, www.carnforthstation.co.uk*, has found a special place in English romantic mythology. It was originally an important junction linking the London–Glasgow and Carnforth–Leeds railway but is more commonly known as the set for David Lean's film *Brief Encounter* starring Celia Johnson and Trevor Howard. There is a trail around the station so you can follow the camera positions. The station has undergone extensive renovation after falling into disuse, and you can now use it to reach stations in the Lakes and Lancaster as well as a location to conduct brief affairs yourself. The **Heritage Centre** ① *daily 1000-1600*, houses a collection of advertising posters from 1845 to 1945 and a tribute to David Lean.

The Pendle Witches

In 1612 under the reign of Protestant King James I, the greatest number of witches ever caught were found in the Pendle area and hung at Lancaster Castle. James was obsessed with witchcraft, and the Catholic area of Lancashire was seen as a hotbed for this kind of heresy. The Pendle witchcraft trials centred on two peasant families headed by two old crones, Demdike and Chattox. They were believed to have magic powers, and their daughters and sons likewise, using them to do harm and to consort with the devil. Many locals testified to their evil-doings and, most remarkably of all, the witches confessed to their crimes unlike in other trials of the time. One of the witches, the wonderfully named Alice Nutter, was convicted on the evidence of a nine-year-old child. Her grave is in nearby Newchurch where the graveyard has an eye of God in it to prevent her evil harming others.

Witchcraft was also practised in this time in a healing capacity, and local people were paranoid about the existence of witches. Growing bluebells in your garden was said to be a sign of witchcraft, as witches used the flowers to lure fairies to their houses so that they could pick their brains.

Today, the only remaining evidence about the Pendle witches is the transcript of the court proceedings and many stories have been created in the region to fill in the missing background.

The Ribble Valley → *For listings, see pages 90-93.*

The east of Lancashire is an undiscovered gem, with wonderful walking trails around the Forest of Bowland, charming stone cottages and country pubs. With more of the feel of rural Yorkshire, it all seems a lot further away from the old industrial towns of south Lancashire than it really is. Pendle Hill dominates the area, with the town of Clitheroe and its 12th-century castle. The area is well known in the county as the home of the Pendle Witches, hung in 1612 at Lancaster Castle (see page 85). From Clitheroe you can follow their path around the district. Alongside the River Ribble around Clitheroe you can also follow geology and sculpture trails in the open countryside. The Forest of Bowland is an Area of Outstanding Natural Beauty with many walking and cycle trails.

Arriving in the Ribble Valley
Getting there The town of Clitheroe is seven miles north of Blackburn on the A666/A59. There is a train station in Clitheroe with a regular service to Blackburn and Manchester every day but Sunday. Local buses run to the town from Preston, Bury, Skipton in Yorkshire and Manchester. By far the most convenient way to explore this area of Lancashire is by car, which allows you to reach the more out-of-the-way spots.
→ *See Transport, page 93.*

Tourist information The main information points for the region are **Clitheroe TIC** ①
Ribble Borough Council Offices, Church Walk, T01200-425566, www.visitribblevalley.co.uk,
Mon-Sat 0900-1700, and **Clitheroe Visitor Centre** ① *Platform Gallery, Station Rd.* The
website www.visitclitheroe.co.uk also has some useful visitor information.

Clitheroe

Clitheroe is a small country town presided over by a 12th-century **Norman castle** with an
unusual hole in the wall of its keep. The town has an array of pubs and a few places to stay
as well as a charming arts and crafts gallery in a refurbished railway building.

Climb up the steep and winding path around the formal garden and you will reach the
keep of **Clitheroe Castle** ① *Castle St, T01200-424568, free.* It was built in 1186 by Robert
De Lacy to protect his estate and is made of limestone and sandstone. There's a great view
of Pendle Hill from 35 m above the limestone bed as well as the surrounding rural area.
Housed in one of the Georgian stone buildings in the courtyard behind the castle, the
Castle Museum ① *T01200-424568, Apr-Oct daily 1100-1600, Nov-Apr daily 1200-1600,*
£3.75, concessions £2.85, children free, was recently refurbished and now houses
interesting displays that take you through 350 million years of local history, including the
Pendle witches, geology and a sound system to provide an authentic experience of life in
an Edwardian kitchen. Upstairs is a reconstructed 18th-century lead mine with whistling
and coughing miners to keep you company.

Modern arts and crafts are on display at the **Platform Gallery** ① *Station Rd, Clitheroe,*
T0120 0-443071, www.platformgallery.org.uk, Mon-Sat 1000-1630, free, in a refurbished
railway building next door to the train station. The changing exhibitions feature ceramics,
sculpture, design, paintings and felt work in an intimate quirky space. The contemporary
crafts are mainly produced by local artists based in the Northwest.

Forest of Bowland → *www.forestofbowland.com.*

The Forest of Bowland is not so much a forest as a remote area of deep valleys, barren
gritstone fells and peat moorland that was once part of an ancient wilderness stretching
as far as the New Forest. It's popular with walkers and cyclists though it receives relatively
few visitors. Just eight miles from Clitheroe, the **Bowland Wild Boar Park** ① *2 miles from*
Chipping village on the Chipping–Dunsop Bridge road, T01995-61554,
www.wildboarpark.co.uk, Easter-end Oct daily 1030-1700, £5.50, concessions/child £5,
Nov-Feb daily 1100-1600, consists of 65 acres of woodland with wild boars, longhorn cows
and deer roaming freely. In the spring you can hand-feed the lambs, and it's a great area
for picnics.

Walking trails around Clitheroe

Pendle Witches Trail The TIC in Clitheroe sells guides to this 45-mile route which
traces the path taken by the 10 convicted witches from the Pendle area to their final
destination at Lancaster Castle. Begin at **Pendle Heritage Centre** ① *Park Hill, Barrowford,*
Nelson, T01282-661701, www.visitpendle.com. It's a 17th-century hall with a video about
the witches which will start you off. The trail continues via a number of small country
towns and Clitheroe to Lancaster Castle; contact the TIC for further details.

Walks in the Northwest

The Northwest has some excellent short- and long-distance walking paths.
The Pennine Way The Peak District (see page 44). Starting at Edale, head south for Mam Tor or north for Kinder Scout. *OS Landranger 110*.
The Grindsbrook Path The Peak District (see page 45). A well-worn walking trail that eventually turns into the Pennine Way. *OS Landranger 110*.

The Roman Walls Chester (see page 58). A 40-minute tour of the town and the best way to get your bearings.
Ribble Valley Sculpture Trail Brungerley Park by Clitheroe, in Lancashire (see below).
The Way of the Gull Isle of Man (see page 100). Starting at Peel, this 90-mile path heads out along the shoreline round the island. *OS Landranger 95*.

Geology Trail Salthill Quarry near Clitheroe has provided the town with limestone for the last 300 years and was reclaimed in 1980 as a geology trail. The limestone rocks here date back to 300 million years ago when Britain lay at the equator. The route along the trail is punctuated with signboards telling you about the rocks and the creatures that lived in the basin, such as corals and sponges. The trail starts and ends at the Salthill industrial estate just off Lincoln Way just on the edge of Clitheroe town and has well-marked footpaths throughout.

Ribble Valley Sculpture Trail This can be found in Brungerley Park just outside Clitheroe on the B6478 towards Waddington and takes you across a part of the Ribble Way from Brungerley Bridge to Crosshill Quarry following sculptures based around the natural environment. The entrance is marked from the road, and the artists have made the most of natural features like hollow tree trunks and fungus to create an interesting trail.

The Ribble Way The Ribble Way is a 70-mile long path along the River Ribble from its source to the estuary. You can pick up the trail at various locations and it takes you through limestone gorges, marshland and moorland. The best map to take for the area is the *OS Explorer OSL41 Forest of Bowland and Ribblesdale* and further information about the path can be found at Clitheroe TIC.

Lancashire listings

For hotel and restaurant price codes and other relevant information, see pages 9-12.

⊜ Where to stay

Blackpool *p82, map p83*

There are an enormous number of B&Bs in Blackpool, some of which conform to the stereotype of grotty rooms, greasy breakfasts and over-bearing landladies. Beware also of stag nights and hen parties in your guesthouse or hotel. In recent years the standard of accommodation has improved, with a couple of luxury 5-star boutique guesthouses and a scattering of business hotels.

££££-£££ Number One South Beach, 4 Harrowside West, just south of the Pleasure Beach, T01253-343900, www.numberone southbeach.com. The plushest place to stay in town with 14 luxury rooms with king-size or 4-poster beds, plasma TV, en suite bathroom with whirlpool tub and music system. Each room is individually styled and some have a balcony overlooking the sea. The bar and restaurant offer an elegant alternative to the rest of Blackpool. The sister guesthouse, **Number One St Luke's** is equally luxurious and located a few streets away at 1 St Lukes Rd, South Shore, www.numberoneblackpool.com.

£££-££ Big Blue Hotel, Pleasure Beach, T0871-222 4000, www.bigbluehotel.com. Living up to its name, you can't miss this smart modern hotel with 157 rooms in neutral tones and with all mod cons.

££ Derwent Hotel, 42 Palatine Rd, T01253-620004, www.derwenthotelblackpool.co.uk. Small 11-bedroomed family hotel with en suite bathrooms and welcoming friendly hosts. Dinner is available as well as B&B.

££ Raffles Hotel, 73-75 Hornby Rd, T01253-294713, www.raffleshotelblackpool.co.uk. Smart, very English hotel with top service. Friendly and pleasant.

££-£ Beachcomber Hotel, 78 Read's Av, T01253-621622, www.beachcomber hotel.net. Family guesthouse with small rooms, a restaurant and car park.

££-£ The Granville Hotel, 12 Station Rd, T01253-343012, www.granvillehotel.com. Pleasant small hotel catering particularly for families and groups, with en suite bathrooms, a licensed bar and home-cooked meals.

££-£ Manor Grove Hotel, 24 Leopold Grove, T01253-625577, http://themanorgrove.co.uk. Friendly hotel/guesthouse with cosy rooms, standard B&B and an evening meal if required.

£ Carlton Hotel, 64 Albert Rd, T01253-622693, www.thecarlton.com. Small, well-kept 3-star hotel in central Blackpool, with en suite bathrooms and a seaside atmosphere. Pets welcome.

Lancaster *p85*

Lancaster is a great place to base yourself if you are touring the Northwest or for a stop on the way to the Lake District.

££££-£££ The Ashton, Wyresdale Rd, T01524-68460, www.theashtonlancaster.com. If you fancy staying outside the city itself, this sumptuous B&B makes a great base for exploring the area. Rooms are smart with flatscreen TVs and immaculate decor. There's a small sitting room, and breakfast is provided by the chickens in the garden.

£££-££ Penny Street Bridge, Penny St, T01524-599900, www.pennystreet bridge.co.uk. Right in the heart of the city, this grand pub-hotel with 28 rooms has been refurbished to a high standard yet retains its original features with high ceilings, stained glass windows and art deco lights. Good restaurant downstairs.

£££-££ The Sun Hotel and Bar, 63-65 Church St, T01524-66006, www.thesun hotelandbar.co.uk. 16 smart en suite rooms in a traditional 17th-century inn with a warm and cosy atmosphere. Bar and restaurant downstairs.

££ Greenbank Farmhouse, Abbeystead, T01524-792063, www.greenbankfarm house.co.uk. Stone farmhouse just outside Lancaster in the rolling countryside, 15 mins from the city centre at junction 3 of the M6. Well-kept grounds, good location for walking and fishing and a wonderful personal touch.

££ Royal Kings Arms, 75 Market St, T0843-178 7161, www.bespokehotels.com/royalkingsarmshotel. A 3-star period hotel on one of Lancaster's wide cobbled streets, the **King's Arms** is modern, relaxed and welcoming. Charles Dickens stayed here in 1854 and 1862, and although much of the interior has been modernized, the stained-glass windows and features like the minstrel's gallery remain.

££ Shakespeare Hotel, 96 St Leonards Gate, T01524-841041, www.theshakespeare lancaster.co.uk. Popular and award-winning B&B on the outskirts of town with top-class service.

Ribble Valley *p87*

There are plenty of lovely places to stay in the scenic Ribble Valley and it's a relaxing place to spend a few days, especially if you're into walking.

££££-£££ Mitton Hall Country House Hotel, Mitton Rd, Whalley, near Clitheroe, T01254-826544, www.mittonhallhotel.co.uk. Grand and beautiful old country house with historic interior, large fireplace, lovingly decorated with antlers, and antique furniture. There are 4-poster beds for the ultimate in romance and luxury; golfing, fishing and executive breaks also catered for.

£££-££ Red Pump Inn, Clitheroe Rd, Bashall Eaves, T01254-826227, www.thered pumpinn.co.uk. Attractive rural pub with comfortable guest bedrooms, top notch food available in the restaurant downstairs.

£££-££ The Spread Eagle, Sawley, Clitheroe, T01200-441202, www.spread eaglesawley.co.uk. This stylish Lancashire inn on the banks of the Ribble has 7 spacious comfortable rooms, some with views over the river, and superb food.

££ Brooklyn Guesthouse, 32 Pimlico Rd, Clitheroe, T01200-428268, www.brooklyn guesthouse.co.uk. Warm, homely 3-bedroomed Victorian B&B on the outskirts of Clitheroe near to the train station. Rooms are large, comfortable and en suite.

££ Inn at the Station, King St, Clitheroe, T01200-425464, www.innatthestation.co.uk. Newly refurbished B&B above a stone pub in the centre of Clitheroe, home-made bar meals and evening meal by arrangement.

££ Old Post House Hotel, 44-48 King St, Clitheroe, T01200-422025, www.post househotel.co.uk. Family-run townhouse in the centre of Clitheroe town with cosy and charming decor and friendly service.

££ Peter Barn Country House, Cross Lane/Rabbit Lane, Waddington, 4 miles from Clitheroe, T01200-428585, www.peterbarn.co.uk. 18th-century barn conversion with 3 guest rooms overlooking the lovely garden. 2-night minimum stay.

££ Waddington Arms, Waddington, T01200-423262, www.waddingtonarms.co.uk. Old coaching inn, now with comfortable guest rooms, decent food and local ales. Excellent walking right from the doorstep.

🍴 Restaurants

Blackpool *p82, map p83*
It used to be the case that if you were looking for gourmet dinners and elegant restaurants, you took a wrong turning somewhere. Fish and chips is still the standard fare, but a couple of gastro options have now emerged.

£££-££ Number One South Beach, 4 Harrowside West, just south of the Pleasure Beach, T01253-343900, www.numberone southbeach.com. Upmarket dining in a intimate atmosphere. Extensive wine list.

££ Kwizeen, 47-49 King St, T01253-290045, www.kwizeenrestaurant.co.uk. Tasteful restaurant with cream walls, polished wooden floors and jazz playing in the background. Simple menu with big, bold flavours. Aims to source its products as locally as possible, mostly within a 30-mile radius.
££ La Fontana, 17 Clifton St, T01253-622231, www.lafontanarestaurant.co.uk. Family-run Italian restaurant with extensive menu. Charming service and lively atmosphere.
££-£ Blues Bar & Brasserie, Pleasure Beach, T0871-222 4000, www.bigbluehotel.com. Contemporary brasserie and bar with leather armchairs and relaxed ambience. A la carte meals for the grown-ups while children can create their own pizza.
££-£ Ocean Palace, 43 Talbot Rd, T01253-292118 www.oceanpalaceblackpool.co.uk. A decent Chinese option with standard dishes and a takeaway service.

Fish and chip shops
There is very little difference between the shops below apart from **Harry Ramsden's**, 60 Promenade, T01253-393529, the fish and chip shop chain offering a proper sit-down meal and a hiked-up price for the privilege. For all others you should be able to eat for around £5 a head.

Lancaster *p85*
Lancaster is a university town and has a number of pubs, snack bars and fast food places to eat out.
£££ The Castle Restaurant, Royal Kings Arms Hotel (see Where to stay), Market St. Large wine list, good service and traditional English food served in this historic hotel overlooked by a minstrel's gallery. The best place to eat out in Lancaster.
££ Pizza Margherita, 2 Moor Lane, T01524-36333, www.pizza-margherita.co.uk. A large, airy and bright Italian operating as a café, bar and restaurant. It's the classiest of the Italian restaurants in the town.

££ The Sun Hotel and Bar, 63-65 Church St, T01524-66006, www.thesunhoteland bar.co.uk. A traditional pub serving home-cooked food in a warm and cosy atmosphere.
£ The Old John O'Gaunt at 53 Market St Particularly recommended is this quaint and charming pub with stained-glass windows, snugs, stuffed birds and pictures of jazz legends on the walls. They serve traditional pub food and real ale and boast of having "strange staff". You'll have to find out what that means yourself.

Ribble Valley *p87*
£££ Free Masons, 8 Vicarage Fold, Wiswell, Clitheroe, T01254-822218, www.freemasons atwiswell.com. Rural inn with elegant decor including antique rugs and period paintings. The menu is proper gastro fair with unusual cuts of meat and tempting desserts.
££ Red Pump Inn, Clitheroe Rd, Bashall Eaves, T01254-826227, www.theredpump inn.co.uk. Historic inn dating back to 1756, with a reputation for its rustic atmosphere and varied seasonal menu.
££ Three Fishes, T01254-826888, Mitton Rd, Mitton, www.thethreefishes.com. True English pub with log fires and a beer garden. Serves British classics and local specials such as Lancashire hotpot and potted Morecombe Bay shrimps.
££-£ Duke of York Inn, Brow Top, Grindleton, Clitheroe, T01200-441266, www.dukeofyorkgrindleton.com. Low ceilings and stone-flagged floors, this 19th-century inn serves beautifully presented plates of traditional British dishes, full of flavour.
£ The Apricot Meringue, 15 King St, Clitheroe, T01200-426933, www.apricot meringue.co.uk. Elegant teashop just off the high street serving high tea, home-made cakes and vegetarian dishes.
£ Bashall Barn, Bashall Town, Clitheroe, T01200-428964, www.bashallbarn.co.uk. On the road out of Clitheroe towards Bashall, this

dairy barn has been converted into a café, craft workshop and walking centre serving home-cooked snacks out in the country. A cheerful place for a stop while you're walking in the area and a good rain shelter.

£ Halfpenny's of Clitheroe, Old Toll House, 1-5 Parson Lane, Clitheroe, T01200-424478. Listed building housing a traditional English teashop serving sandwiches, roasts, cream teas and pastries. Welcoming and homely.

☺ Pubs, bars and clubs

Lancaster *p85*
The Borough, 3 Dalton Sq, T01524-64170, www.theboroughlancaster.co.uk. Characterful pub in a Grade II-listed building, formerly the Mayor of Lancaster's house. Offers a good selection of local ales and food including hog roasts and a Lancashire platter. Also hosts the **Lancaster Comedy Club**.
The Sun, 63-65 Church St, T01524-66006, www.thesunhotelandbar.co.uk. Lovely old bar with a wide selection of cask ales and wines. Warm hospitality and rarely empty.

⊖ Transport

Lancaster *p85*
Bus
By bus there are twice-hourly services to **Preston** (1 hr 10 mins), **Blackpool** (1 hr 15 mins) and **Kendal** (1 hr 20 mins), **Windermere** (1 hr 30 mins) and **Keswick** (2 hrs 30 mins) in the Lake District.

Train
From Lancaster there are regular train services to **Preston** (25 mins) where you can change for **Liverpool** (1 hr), **Manchester** (45 mins) and **London** (2 hrs 40 mins). You can also reach **Carnforth** (10 mins) by rail.

Ribble Valley *p87*
From Clitheroe it is easy to reach the Yorkshire Dales and towns to the south of Lancashire by road.

Bicycle
The Ribble Valley area has a number of cycle trails through the countryside. The only cycle hire in the area is at **Pedal Power**, Waddington Rd, Clitheroe, T01200-422066, www.pedalpowerclitheroe.co.uk. Mon-Fri 0900-1730, Sat 0900-1630, closed Sun. They can advise on nearby cycle routes through the Forest of Bowland and the Ribble Valley.

Bus
Local buses run to **Accrington** (35 mins), **Manchester** (1 hr 25 mins), **Blackburn** (35 mins), **Bolton** (1 hr 15 mins) and **Preston** (35 mins). For further information about rail and bus services in the region, T01200-429832.

Train
There are regular trains to **Blackburn** (20 mins), **Blackpool** (1 hr 15 mins) and **Manchester** (1 hr 15 mins).

The Isle of Man

The Isle of Man is a place of its own in many different ways. It's a self-governing kingdom, an island a mere 33 miles long and 13 miles wide that lies 60 miles off the Lancashire coast in the Irish Sea. It's classified as a 'crown dependency', neither belonging to the UK nor the EU, with its own parliament, laws, traditions, stamps, currency and language. Everyone in the country speaks English, however, and English money is accepted.

But, like the Bee Gees who hail from this part of the world, the island is often unfairly stereotyped and ridiculed when it should be celebrated for retaining its eccentricity. Perhaps the island is stuck behind in the 1950s, a haven for tax dodgers, while the rest of the UK is hip, modern and trail-blazing. Perhaps the kudos of being the venue for the world's most prestigious motorcycle race is somewhat marred by the fact that it also holds the World Tin Bath Championships. But forget all the criticisms and accolades for a moment and take the time to look at the scenery. There are grouse moors and mountains, wide romantic beaches and leafy woodland dells, ruined castles and an ancient stone circle. The scenery is a microcosm of the British Isles and glorious sunsets in Port Erin and Peel emphasize the Isle of Man's natural isolation.

Arriving on the Isle of Man → *For listings, see pages 101-105.*

Getting there The Isle of Man Airport ① *Ballasalla, T01624-821600, www.iom-airport.com*, also known as Ronaldsway Airport, is 10 miles south of Douglas near Castletown in the southeast of the island. It has good links with many major airports in the UK, Channel Islands, Ireland and further afield with airlines such as **easyJet**, **Flybe**, **City Wing**, **Aer Lingus** and **British Airways** operating daily flights. The small airport is well served by local buses into Douglas and there are a number of car hire operatives.

If you want to take your car to the island, the **Steam Packet Company** ① *T01624-661661, www.steampacket.com, single/return £15/30, car and 2 passengers return £138*, runs car ferry crossings across the rough stretch of the Irish Sea from Heysham, Liverpool, Dublin and Belfast into Douglas taking around 2½ hours. A fast service is available between March and November from Liverpool, Dublin and Belfast. Booking in advance for cheaper deals is recommended. ▸▸ *See Transport, page 105.*

Getting around
The Isle of Man has a good regular bus network, **Bus Vannin**, which serves the whole Island including Ronaldsway Airport and the Sea Terminal in Douglas. Tickets and timetables are available from main bus and railway stations and the Welcome Centre at the Sea Terminal. Multi-journey tickets include the **Island Explorer** (one-day adult £10, child £5, three-day £20, child £10), which allows unlimited travel on all public transport, including the tram to Snaefell and Douglas Horse Trams. See www.iombusandrail.info for more information.

In the south of the country from Douglas to Castletown, Port St Mary and Port Erin there is a rail link with old steam trains that inspired the *Thomas the Tank Engine* stories. From Douglas to Laxey and Ramsey in the north there is an electric railway link and it is possible to reach the top of the island's highest mountain, Snaefell, on the Snaefell Mountain Railway.

However, hiring a car is one of the best ways of exploring the island, especially if you want to discover the glens. The centre of the Isle of Man is only barely reachable by road and is mainly uninhabited. Beware of motorcyclists – even outside the TT season there are more around than you would expect. Bicycle hire is available in Douglas and Ramsey for exploring the island in a more leisurely fashion. Surprisingly, you cannot hire a motorbike on the Isle of Man due to licence restrictions.

Tourist information
The main visitor information point is the **Welcome Centre** at the Sea Terminal in Douglas (see page 96) but there are smaller TICs in some of the main towns and villages. The websites www.iomguide.com and www.isleofman.com are also useful.

Background

The Isle of Man was inhabited by hunter-gatherers from 8000 BC to 4500 BC and has a rich and varied political and cultural history. In slightly more recent times the Celts lived here, an era of myths and legends backed up by archaeological evidence found on St Patrick's Isle in Peel and a number of beautiful carved stone crosses. The Isle of Man was never ruled by the Romans or the Anglo-Saxons and was Christianized during the fifth and sixth centuries by Irish monks. Around the year AD 800, the Norwegian Vikings appeared and settled on the island, which provided them with a good base for raiding and trading around the Irish Sea. The Kingdom of the Sudreys was established in the AD 970s, consisting of the Isle of Man and the Western Isles of Scotland. It was ruled over by the Tynwald, the Viking age parliament established on the Isle of Man which still exists today and is the oldest continuous national parliament in the world.

The Kingdom of the Sudreys was under threat from the Scots and finally dissolved in 1265 with the death of Norse King Magnus III in Castletown. The Scots ruled the island briefly at this point until 1290 when England took over. Between 1290 and 1333 it came under English and Scots rule alternately until, finally, the battle between the two powers at Hallidon Hill resolved the issue: the Isle of Man was to be kept under the sovereignty of the English Crown and ruled by English noblemen.

Tourism became popular in the 19th century and reached a peak in 1899 attracting a combination of working class people from Scotland and the North of England as well as the wealthier classes. In the next few years the advent of the motor car and motor car racing on the Isle of Man began to bring even more enthusiasts over as the sport was less regulated on the island than on the stricter mainland. The Isle of Man did not escape the Depression in the 1930s, and the country's lead, copper and zinc mines were abandoned. With the Second World War, the island was again involved in war as a prisoner of war camp and internment centre. It was said at the time that the only casualties on the island during this time were a rabbit and a frog, killed by a German jettisoning his bombs! Since the Second World War the island has seen political, social and economic changes but still governs itself, albeit with close connections to Westminster.

Places on the Isle of Man

Douglas

The Victorian seaside resort of Douglas is the administrative and banking capital of the island as well as being its main hub for hotels and shops. A sandy beach lies at the foot of a sweeping promenade still busy with 19th-century horse-drawn trams. It isn't as pretty as the island's other towns, but it's the most developed and has many restaurants and hotels.

Tourist information The **Welcome Centre** ① *Sea Terminal Building, T01624-686766, www.visitisleofman.com, daily May-Sep, closed Sun Oct-Apr,* is the central information point for the island. A 10-day **Heritage Explorer Ticket** (£18, child £9) is available from the Welcome Centre or online at www.manxheritageshop.com, and allows unlimited free entry to the Castle Rushen, Old House of Keys, Nautical Museum, Rushen Abbey, Cregneash National Folk Museum, Peel Castle, House of Mananann, Grove Museum and the Laxey Wheel, as well as discounts at a number of other attractions.

The **Manx Museum** ⓘ *Kingswood Grove, T01624-648000, www.manxnationalheritage.im, Mon-Sat 1000-1700, free,* contains the National Art Gallery (with works by Archibald Knox, William Hoggat and John Miller Nicholson), geology, archaeology, social history and TT race displays. It also has some beautiful glass beads believed to belong to a Viking noblewoman found at Peel Castle. Allow a couple of hours to explore the museum thoroughly. It's the best place in Douglas to escape the rain and entertain children with fairy folklore and multimedia displays.

Just two miles out of the town past the suburb of Onchan is the **Groudle Glen Railway** ⓘ *the glen is 2 miles along the coast road from Douglas to Laxey, www.ggr.org.uk, trains run May-Sep every half hour Sun 1100-1630, Jul-Aug trains also run Wed 1900-2100, return £4, child £2, discounts if combined with Manx Electric Railway,* a late Victorian narrow-gauge railway service that takes you down through beautiful woodland and beach scenery to Sea Lion Rocks.

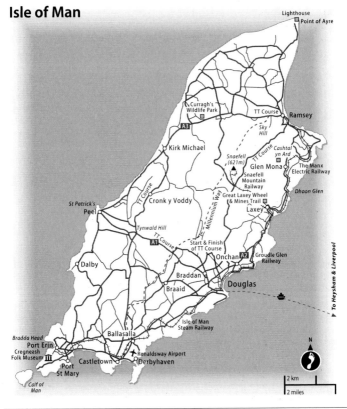

Isle of Man

Around the island

An hour by bus from Douglas, **Castletown**, a large village with a beach and pretty harbour in the south of the island, is dominated by the large **Castle Rushen** ① *The Quay, T01624-648000, www.manxnationalheritage.im, Mar-Nov daily 1000-1600, Jun-Aug open until 1700, £5.80, child £3*, which dates back to the 12th century and is one of Europe's best preserved medieval castles. The limestone fortress was the home of the former Kings and Lords of Mann, including the last Norse monarch, King Magnus in 1265. Having been an administrative centre, prison and law court amongst other things in the past, it is now a fabulous museum. Walking around the walls and down to the dungeons is well worth it. The **Old Grammar School** ① *Chapel Lane, T01624-648017, www.manxnationalheritage.im, Apr-Nov daily 1000-1600, Jul-Aug until 1700, free*, was built as the church for the settlement that grew up around the castle and dates back to AD 1200. It's the oldest roofed structure on the island and older than many parts of the castle. It was used as a school from 1570 to 1930 and houses a preserved Victorian classroom complete with old-fashioned desks and blackboard. The long and turbulent history of the Isle of Man's political independence is explored in the **Old House of Keys** ① *Old House of Keys, Parliament Sq, T01624-648000, Mar-Nov daily 1000-1700, 45-min guided presentations run on the hour, £4.50, child £2.25*. It has been restored to its 1866 glory as the parliament house and debating chamber.

Port St Mary and **Port Erin**, charming neighbouring coastal towns at the south of the island, are often called the sisters of the south. Port St Mary is a quaint and pretty place with a small harbour and beach that's perfect for rockpooling. A walk along the coast beside the palm trees for about five minutes takes you to **Chapel Beach**, a sandy stretch just a little out of the way. Along the coast in the other direction will take you to the cliffs and the **Chasms**, dramatic vertical rifts in the rocks. Not far from the town is the **Cregneash Folk Museum** ① *Cregneash, Port St Mary, T01624-648000, Mar-Nov daily 1000-1600, Jun-Aug open until 1700, £4.50, child £2.25*, which represents the way that crofters lived and worked in the 19th century.

From Port Erin, just eight miles from Port St Mary on the west coast, a walk up **Bradda Head** is worth doing on a nice day where you'll find the perfect place to watch the sun set. **Erin Arts Centre** ① *Victoria Sq, T01624-836658, www.erinartscentre.com, open year round Tue-Fri 1300-1630, prices for events differ*, acts as a small art gallery to display local work and a venue for opera, touring shows and theatre. Daily boat trips from Port Erin take you to the bird sanctuary of **Calf Island**, a 616-acre islet off the southern tip of the Isle of Man. Transport to the Calf is by boat from Port St Mary with **Calf Island Cruises** ① *Raglan Pier, T01624-832339, Apr-Oct weather permitting, 1015, 1130 and 1300*. The **Sound Visitor Centre** ① *Sound Rd, Port St Mary, T01624-838123, Nov-Mar Mon-Fri 1000-1600, weekends 1000-1700, Apr-Oct 1000-sunset*, has displays on local history including the Calf of Man and includes a large café built into the headland with panoramic views.

These days, **Peel** is the main fishing town on the island; it is also one of the oldest cathedral cities in the British Isles, dating back to the sixth century. Its narrow winding streets are historic and pretty if you overlook the ugly power station and chimney at the top of the town. The unmissable **House of Manannan** ① *Mill Rd, T01624-648000, daily 1000-1700, £6, child £3*, is a multimedia feast of Viking, Celtic and Manx history with sights, sounds, talking waterfalls and excellent short films bringing each period alive. **Peel Castle** ① *West Quay, T01624-648017, Mar-Nov daily 1000-1600, Aug-Sep open until 1700, £4.50, child £2.25*, stands on **St Patrick's Isle**, which has been used as a fortress since the Celtic Iron

The three legs of Man

The three legs of Man aren't a representation of a genetic mutation or the island's fairy heritage but a symbol of the island's independence. The symbol is displayed on houses, tourist attractions and flags all over the island and the Latin legend beneath it translates as "Whichever way you throw me I stand." Many nations have risen to the challenge from the Vikings to the English but the Isle of Man remains self-governing, with the Tynwald parliament the oldest continuous parliament in the world.

Age and was a former Viking stronghold. The crumbling sandstone walls enclose an 11th-century church and round tower, St Germain's Cathedral and the ruins of the later apartments of the Lords of Mann. The island used to be completely cut off from the mainland at high tide but when the causeway was built to link the island a small sandy beach, Fenella's Beach, was created naturally on one side. On the road from Peel to Douglas, the **Tynwald Hill** is the site of the oldest continuous parliament in the world. The name derives from the Norse word *Thing-voeller* meaning Parliament Fields, and the site is a small circular area of stepped grass crowned with a flag.

The mountain of **Snaefell** is one of the highlights of the Isle of Man. At 2036 ft Snaefell means 'Snow Mountain' and it is said that from the top of the mountain you can see the six kingdoms: England, Ireland, Scotland, Wales, Mann and the Kingdom of Heaven. You can reach the top by walking all the way, taking the tram halfway and walking the rest or by taking the 100-year-old **mountain railway** ① *Laxey Station, T01624-663366, Apr-Nov, journeys take 30 mins, fares from Laxey to the summit return £10, child £5*, all the way to the top. There's a small café at the top to rest yourself or commiserate when all you can see is a large blanket of mist.

The megalithic standing stones at **Cashtal yn Ard** are thought to mark a burial ground and stand in an eerie part of the country. Follow the A2 road from Laxey north past Dhoon Glen and then take the next right after Glen Mona. The standing stones are on the left-hand side of the road. Whilst in the Laxey area, it's worth visiting the **Laxey Wheel** ① *off Mine's Rd, Mar-Nov daily 0900-1600, Jun-Aug open until 1700*, the world's largest working waterwheel. Dating back to 1854, it's an impressive feat of engineering.

Walks on the island

The Millennium Way In 1979 to commemorate 100 years of the Tynwald parliament, the Millennium Way was established as the first long-distance footpath on the island. It is based on the Royal Way recorded by the monks of Rushen in the 14th century and takes in both historical and natural points of interest in its 28 miles. It can be walked by an experienced hiker in one day or you can split it into three legs. Starting from the main road to Kirk Michael from Ramsey, approximately one mile from Ramsey Town Square, the route climbs up towards Sky Hill, site of the 1079 battle between the Norse King Godred and the Manx, which the Scandinavians won. The way continues down around the stream at the foot of Snaefell and finishes at Castletown after traversing the countryside and Norse landmarks between. Maps and close descriptions of the walk can be found at the Welcome Centre (see page 96).

The Way of the Gull A coast path runs 90 miles along the northern shore from Peel right around the island, marked with a sign with the silhouette of a gull. It takes about four days to complete. The walk follows a disused railway line from Peel to the beach at the bottom of Glen Trunk at Orrisdale. From there it follows the beach past the lighthouse at the Point of Ayre through to Ramsey, down to Douglas and beyond to Castletown. From here the Chasms at Port St Mary are visited, vertical rifts in the cliffs, providing excellent views of the Calf of Man. The walk finishes at Contrary Head where the tide divides, one part flowing southwest to the Calf and the other northeast to Jerby. A full description and further information is available from the Welcome Centre (see page 96).

The Isle of Man listings

For hotel and restaurant price codes and other relevant information, see pages 9-12.

🛏 Where to stay

Douglas p96

££££-£££ The Claremont, 18-22 Loch Promenade, T01624-698800, www.clare monthoteldouglas.com. Young, modern seafront hotel with 28 luxury rooms, modern pine-floored designer bar and restaurant serving Mediterranean and French food.

££££-£££ Mount Murray Hotel and Country Club, Mount Murray Rd, Santon, T01624-661111, www.mountmurray.com. Just out of Douglas, the island's most luxurious timbered hotel with a full health complex, golf course and acres of beautiful scenery.

£££ Acacia Boutique Hotel, Marathon Terrace, Queens Promenade, T01624-660600, www.acaciaboutique.co.uk. Stylish rooms in this contemporary seafront hotel which incorporates some original Victorian features. All mod cons. **Manila Café and Restaurant** downstairs.

£££ Sefton Hotel, Harris Promenade, T01624-645500, www.seftonhotel.co.im. Large spacious and classy seafront hotel with leisure club, cycle hire and library. The restaurant serves Manx specials, and rooms are comfortable with sofas and fridges. Relaxing, hospitable and luxurious.

£££ The Welbeck Hotel, Mona Dr, off Central Promenade, T01624-675663, www.welbeckhotel.com. Small, traditional, family-run, relaxed hotel-guesthouse just off the promenade with bar, restaurant and gym.

£££-££ The Empress Hotel, Central Promenade, T01624-661155, www.the empresshotel.net. Grand Victorian seafront hotel with a health club, marble bathrooms, a high standard of service and a fine sea view.

££ Admiral House Hotel, 12 Loch Promenade, T01624-629551, www.admiral house.com. Luxury seafront hotel with excellent service and a choice of modern rooms or 4-poster-bed suites. Also a bar serving food and a Mediterranean restaurant in the basement.

££ Hydro Hotel, Queen's Promenade, T01624-676870, www.hydrohotel.co.im. Large traditional Victorian hotel with a cosy bistro and great view of the seafront.

££ The Savoy, Central Promenade, T07624-406000, www.savoyiom.com. Small family-run, traditional, English seaside hotel. Open the door and you're practically on the beach.

Camping

Glen Dhoo Campsite, Glen Dhoo Farm, T01624-621254. Medium-sized campsite to the north of Douglas open all year round. Follow the A18 out of Douglas to the north to Hillberry and Glen Dhoo farm. Also has cottages for rent.

Around the Island p98

££ Falcon's Nest Hotel, The Promenade, Port Erin, T01624-834077, www.falconsnesthotel. co.uk. Pleasant family-run hotel just off the promenade with cosy rooms and mod cons. It's above a traditional Manx pub serving local ale in the glow of an open fire. Very friendly.

££ The Grosvenor Hotel, The Promenade, Port Erin, T01624-834124, www.grosvenor hotel.biz. Stylish and attractive small Victorian seafront hotel with views of Bradda Head.

££ Patchwork Guesthouse, Bay View Rd, Port St Mary, T01624-836418, www.patchwork.im. Clean, comfortable rooms with lots of light, in a central location. Hearty breakfast in the café downstairs (see Restaurants).

££ The River House, Ramsey, T01624-816412, www.theriverhouse-iom.com. Small charming Georgian house with a true English country feel, en suite bathrooms and exemplary service.

££ Rowany Cottier Guest House,
Spaldrick near Port Erin, T01624-832287,
www.rowanycottier.com. Spacious, elegant
house with a large garden and extensive
Manx breakfast menu. Family-run with
high-quality service.

££ The Waldick Hotel, Promenade, Peel,
T01624-842410, www.waldickhotel.co.uk.
Friendly family-run hotel on the promenade
in Peel overlooking the beach.

££-£ Ballaquinney Farm, Ronague
near Castletown, T01624-824125. Manx
farmhouse B&B with evening meals in the
countryside near to Castletown.

££-£ Ballasholague Farm, Main Rd, Glen
Mona, T01624-861750. Secluded Edwardian
farmhouse halfway between Ramsey and
Laxey with a farmhouse breakfast and good
walking nearby.

££-£ Beachcroft Guest House,
Beach Rd, Port St Mary, T01624-834521,
www.beachcroftguesthouse.com. Secluded
family-run guesthouse with lovely views of
the surrounding countryside.

££-£ The George Hotel, The Parade,
Castletown, T01624-822533, www.george
hotel.im. Central large traditional Georgian
hotel with comfortable rooms.

**£ Maughold Venture Centre
Bunkhouse**, near Ramsey, T01624-814240,
www.adventure-centre.co.uk. Self-catering
bunkhouse on a converted farm next to the
Venture Centre activity centre which offers a
wide range of outdoor pursuits.

Self-catering and camping

The Coach House, Ballamoar Farm,
Patrick Rd, Patrick Village, T01624-842393,
www.ballamoar-coach-house.com. Beautiful
stone cottage for 4 with wonderful views and
a log-burning fire.

Glenlough Campsite, Ballahutchin Hill,
Union Mills, T01624-852057, www.glenlough
campsite.com. Apr-Oct. A 10-min walk from
the village. Cosy wooden pods available for
those that don't have a tent.

Kionslieu Farm Cottages, Higher Foxdale,
T01624-801349, www.iomfarmholidays.com.
Lovely stone cottages on a traditional farm
with large gardens, friendly animals and a
children's play area. A great option for
families or walkers.

Peel Campsite, T01624-842341,
http://peelonline.net/wheretostay/campsite.
Large campsite open Apr-Nov. Also has
self-catering accommodation on site.

Silly Moos Campsite, Ballakillingan Farm,
Churchtown, Ramsey, T01624-812368,
www.sillymooscampsite.co.uk. Large flat
campsite next to the river. Kitchen, electricity
hook-up, hot showers, and picnic areas.

🍴 Restaurants

Douglas *p96*

£££ The Gallery, Sefton Hotel,
Harris Promenade, T01624-645500,
www.seftonhotel.co.im. High-quality Manx
menu including dishes flambéed at your
table and home-made ice cream.

£££ Stephen Dedman – A Restaurant,
Regency Hotel, Queens Promenade, T01624-
680680, www.regency.im. Oak-panelled
restaurant with a classical feel, decorated with
old photos and pictures. Imaginative menu
including cheese soufflé, Manx queenies and
grilled calves liver.

£££-££ Coast Bar and Brasserie, The
Claremont, 18-22 Loch Promenade, T01624-
617068, www.coast.im. Sophisticated and
spacious art deco restaurant overlooking the
sea. Extensive brasserie-style menu includes a
seafood platter, Manx lamb rump and Baileys
and banana bread and butter pudding.

£££-££ McFarlanes, 24 Duke St,
T01624-624777, www.macfarlanes.im.
Upmarket family-run restaurant in the centre
of town with a simple fresh menu including
pan-seared Manx scallops, McFarlanes fish pie
and a daily blackboard of specials.

£££-££ Tanroagan Seafood Restaurant,
9 Ridgeway St, T01624-612355,

http://tanroagan.co.uk. Grab yourself an Isle of Man crab toastie, Manx seafood gratin, or half a lobster at this small, independent restaurant with a great reputation.

££ Greens Vegetarian Restaurant, Steam Railway Station, North Quay, T01624-629129. Small relaxed vegetarian restaurant-café next to the historic railway station.

££ JAR, Admirals House, 11-12 Loch Promenade, T01624-663553, www.jar.co.im. Tasty Italian-inspired menu in an elegant setting with a leather furnishings. Reasonably priced mains include steaks, seafood and pasta dishes.

££ La Brasserie, Empress Hotel, Central Promenade, T01624-661155, www.theempresshotel.net. French restaurant inside the Empress Hotel which is a copy of an authentic French Brasserie near the Gare du Nord in Paris. Various menus available including a Sunday roast in a stylish and traditional restaurant.

££ La Piazza, Loch Promenade, T01624-672136, www.lapiazza.co.im. Recently refurbished, first floor stylish wooden-floored Italian restaurant open for lunch and evening meals Mon-Sat.

££ La Posada, Admiral House Hotel, 12 Loch Promenade, T01624-629551, www.admiralhouse.com. Basement restaurant specializing in Spanish and Mediterranean food in a warm cantina-style atmosphere.

££ Scotts Bistro, 7 John St, T01624-623764. Smart warm bistro inside the oldest house in Douglas. The bistro specializes in jacket potatoes and other home cooking and has a decent wine list. In the summer you can eat outside in the courtyard. Recommended.

£ Laughing Buddha, Prospect Hill, T01624-673367. Located towards Onchan, specializes in Peking food for lunch, dinner and takeaways. Closed Sun.

Around the island *p98*

£££-££ Abbey, Rushen Abbey, Mill Rd, Ballasalla, T01624-822393, www.theabbeyrestraurant.co.im. Modern European cooking in this attractive tastefully converted abbey with original features. There's a garden room and children's play area at the back.

££ The Marine Hotel, The Promenade, Peel, T01624-842337, www.marinehotelpeel.co.uk. Large pub with a bar and restaurant serving home-cooked food and real ale. If you want the true Manx experience, ask for a kipper dish.

££ The Swiss House Bar & Grill, Glen Helen, St John's, T01624-801657, www.theswisshouse.co.uk. Sister restaurant to **Tanroagan** in Douglas set within the Glen Helen National Park, with a unique charcoal oven for indoor barbecue of meat, fish and vegetables.

££ The Whitehouse, Tynwald Rd, Peel, T01624-842252, www.thewhitehouse peel.com. Manx farmhouse-pub with home cooking, bar snacks and meals and a large range of guest beers as well as the local Okell's brew.

££-£ The Creek Inn, East Quay, Station Place, Peel, T01624-842216, www.thecreek inn.co.uk. Small, cosy central pub with live music and simple dishes served throughout the day. The seafood is particularly good.

£ BarLogo, 39 Parliament St, Ramsey, T01624-813557. One of the Isle of Man's only young, fresh, continental café bars with bar snacks, Mediterranean food and a large range of cocktails.

£ The Old Bakery Café and Restaurant, 31 Malew St, Castletown, T01624-823092. Comfortable and traditional Manx teashop and restaurant in the centre of the town.

£ Timm's Bistro, 5 East St, Ramsey, T01624-817967. Friendly bistro serving Manx food, specializing in seafood.

May TT Festival Fortnight. The world famous Tourist Trophy motorcycle race has been held on the Isle of Man since 1904 and is one of the world's most famous motorsport events. Every year for the last week in May and first week in Jun the island comes alive with passionate fans watching the contenders fly by. The circuit is 37.73 miles long and leading riders can reach speeds of 120 mph/200 kph. If you're planning to watch, accommodation is hard to come by and you are advised to book in advance, www.iomtt.com.

Jun Isle of Music Festival. Festival celebrating the best of the island's music.

Jun Manx National Week. Celebration of Manx culture, language and customs.

End Jun/early Jul Queenie Festival. Celebrates the island's marine heritage, especially the Queen Scallop or 'Queenie'. Starts with a beach party in St Erin and followed up by a marine weekend in Port St Mary.

Jul Tynwald Day. The national day of the Isle of Man.

Jul International Cycling Festival. 5 days of cycling around the island's roads.

Aug Manx Grand Prix. Grand Prix event around the island.

Aug World Tin Bath Championship. In essence, it's one person per tin bath racing against one another across the harbour at Peel to see if anyone can stay afloat long enough to reach the finish line.

Aug World Championship Viking Longboat Races. Viking longboat races remembering a portion of the island's history.

Sep Isle of Man Food and Drink Festival. A celebration of Manx food from smoked kippers to cream teas, with cooking demonstrations by celebrity chefs.

Oct Isle of Man Choir Festival. Attracts choirs from all over the world.

Cycling

The Isle of Man has calm country roads that are well suited to cycling, although you should make sure you keep clear of the TT fortnight at the end of May and beginning of Jun if you want a relaxing experience. The TIC provides a pamphlet on cycling around the island including 6 1-day trails of differing levels around the glens and pretty seaside villages.

Eurocycles, 8a Victoria Rd (off Broadway), Douglas, T01624-624909, www.euro cycles.co.im. Full range of bikes available to buy or hire.

Fishing

For a list of sea, river and reservoir fishing locations, ask at the Welcome Centre in Douglas; they also provide a useful pamphlet and fishing licences which all anglers must have. River fishing runs until the end of Sep, reservoir fishing until the end of Oct and salmon and sea trout fishing is best in late summer/autumn. Freshwater fishing is mainly for salmon, brown and rainbow trout with the occasional sea trout. Douglas Harbour has breakwater and pier fishing, if you're lucky you might land yourself a conger eel.

Outdoor pursuits

The Venture Centre, Lewaigue Farm, Maughold, T01624-814240, www.adventure-centre.co.uk. Outdoor pursuits centre with a whole host of activities from kayaking and coasteering to archery and abseiling.

Pony trekking

Stables are a way out of town and can only be reached by car. Prices from £20 an hr. The website www.horseridingcentres.com/isle_of_man has a list of riding centres.

Abbeylands Equestrian Centre,
Lower Sulby Rd, Scollag Rd, Abbeylands,
T01624-676717.
Ballahimmin Pony Trekking Centre,
Ballahimmin Farm off Little London Rd,
Cronk y Voddy, T01624-482990.
Pennybridge Stables, Main Rd, Kirk Michael,
T01624-878859. For experienced riders only.

Sailing and windsurfing
The Welcome Centre has a pamphlet
detailing all sea-going activities on the island.
The Isle of Man is an ideal place for sailing and
windsurfing whether you're experienced or a
novice. The harbours are picturesque and
there are 6 sailing clubs. Derbyhaven is a
popular spot for windsurfers; contact **Manx
Marine Limited**, Yacht Chandlers, 35 North
Quay, Douglas, T01624-674842,
www.manxmarine.com, for further details.
Douglas Bay Yacht Club, Trafalgar House,
South Quay, Douglas, T01624-621823,
www.douglasbayyachtclub.com.
Isle of Man Yacht Club, Club House,
Lime St, Port St Mary, T01624-832088,
www.iomyc.com.
Manx Sailing and Cruising Club,
North Quay, Ramsey, T01624-813494,
www.msandcc.org.

Walking
The island has some idyllic scenery to walk
through on a number of marked long-
distance footpaths (see TIC pamphlet).
The undulating countryside has sand dunes,
marshland, mountains and meadows of
wild flowers to delight all comers.

⊖ Transport

Douglas *p96*
Air
Aer Lingus, T0871-718 2020 or visit
www.aerlingus.com, flies to **Dublin**. **British
Airways**, T0844-493 0787, www.british

airways.com flies to **London City Airport**.
CityWing, T0871-200 0440, www.city
wing.com, flies to **Anglesey**, **Belfast City**,
Blackpool, **Gloucester**, **Jersey** and
Newcastle. **easyJet**, T08431-041200,
www.easyjet.com, flies to **Liverpool** and
London Gatwick. **Flybe**, T0871-700 2000,
www.flybe.com, flies to **Birmingham**,
Edinburgh, **Glasgow**, **London Gatwick**,
Luton, **Liverpool**, **Manchester** with
seasonal flights to **Jersey** and **Geneva**.

Bus
Bus numbers 4, 5, 6, 8 and 10 run to **Peel**
from the bus station on North Quay; buses
1 and 2 run to **Port St Mary**, **Port Erin**
and **Castletown**.

Car
Athol Garage, Ronaldsway Airport, Ballasalla,
T01624-822481. **E B Christian & Co**, Airport
Garage, Ballasalla, T01624-822126. **Hertz**,
Ronaldsway Airport, Ballasalla, T01624-
823760, www.hertz.co.uk. **Mylchreests Car
Rental**, Ronaldsway Airport, T01624-823533.

Taxi
Laxey Cabs, T07624-432343.

Train
The **Electric Railway** runs from the Derby
Castle stop at the far end of the promenade
to **Ramsey** and **Laxey**, stopping in **Groudle
Glen** and changing at Laxey for the Snaefell
Mountain Railway. Douglas– Castletown–
Port Erin Steam Train (£8.40 return);
Douglas–Laxey–Ramsey Electric Tramway
(£5.20 return); Laxey–Summit Snaefell
Mountain Railway (£7.40 return).

Contents

Footnotes

Index

Notes

Notes

Titles available in the Footprint *Focus* range

Latin America	UK RRP	US RRP
Bahia & Salvador	£7.99	$11.95
Brazilian Amazon	£7.99	$11.95
Brazilian Pantanal	£6.99	$9.95
Buenos Aires & Pampas	£7.99	$11.95
Cartagena & Caribbean Coast	£7.99	$11.95
Costa Rica	£8.99	$12.95
Cuzco, La Paz & Lake Titicaca	£8.99	$12.95
El Salvador	£5.99	$8.95
Guadalajara & Pacific Coast	£6.99	$9.95
Guatemala	£8.99	$12.95
Guyana, Guyane & Suriname	£5.99	$8.95
Havana	£6.99	$9.95
Honduras	£7.99	$11.95
Nicaragua	£7.99	$11.95
Northeast Argentina & Uruguay	£8.99	$12.95
Paraguay	£5.99	$8.95
Quito & Galápagos Islands	£7.99	$11.95
Recife & Northeast Brazil	£7.99	$11.95
Rio de Janeiro	£8.99	$12.95
São Paulo	£5.99	$8.95
Uruguay	£6.99	$9.95
Venezuela	£8.99	$12.95
Yucatán Peninsula	£6.99	$9.95

Asia	UK RRP	US RRP
Angkor Wat	£5.99	$8.95
Bali & Lombok	£8.99	$12.95
Chennai & Tamil Nadu	£8.99	$12.95
Chiang Mai & Northern Thailand	£7.99	$11.95
Goa	£6.99	$9.95
Gulf of Thailand	£8.99	$12.95
Hanoi & Northern Vietnam	£8.99	$12.95
Ho Chi Minh City & Mekong Delta	£7.99	$11.95
Java	£7.99	$11.95
Kerala	£7.99	$11.95
Kolkata & West Bengal	£5.99	$8.95
Mumbai & Gujarat	£8.99	$12.95

Africa & Middle East	UK RRP	US RRP
Beirut	£6.99	$9.95
Cairo & Nile Delta	£8.99	$12.95
Damascus	£5.99	$8.95
Durban & KwaZulu Natal	£8.99	$12.95
Fès & Northern Morocco	£8.99	$12.95
Jerusalem	£8.99	$12.95
Johannesburg & Kruger National Park	£7.99	$11.95
Kenya's Beaches	£8.99	$12.95
Kilimanjaro & Northern Tanzania	£8.99	$12.95
Luxor to Aswan	£8.99	$12.95
Nairobi & Rift Valley	£7.99	$11.95
Red Sea & Sinai	£7.99	$11.95
Zanzibar & Pemba	£7.99	$11.95

Europe	UK RRP	US RRP
Bilbao & Basque Region	£6.99	$9.95
Brittany West Coast	£7.99	$11.95
Cádiz & Costa de la Luz	£6.99	$9.95
Granada & Sierra Nevada	£6.99	$9.95
Languedoc: Carcassonne to Montpellier	£7.99	$11.95
Málaga	£5.99	$8.95
Marseille & Western Provence	£7.99	$11.95
Orkney & Shetland Islands	£5.99	$8.95
Santander & Picos de Europa	£7.99	$11.95
Sardinia: Alghero & the North	£7.99	$11.95
Sardinia: Cagliari & the South	£7.99	$11.95
Seville	£5.99	$8.95
Sicily: Palermo & the Northwest	£7.99	$11.95
Sicily: Catania & the Southeast	£7.99	$11.95
Siena & Southern Tuscany	£7.99	$11.95
Sorrento, Capri & Amalfi Coast	£6.99	$9.95
Skye & Outer Hebrides	£6.99	$9.95
Verona & Lake Garda	£7.99	$11.95

North America	UK RRP	US RRP
Vancouver & Rockies	£8.99	$12.95

Australasia	UK RRP	US RRP
Brisbane & Queensland	£8.99	$12.95
Perth	£7.99	$11.95

For the latest books, e-books and a wealth of travel information, visit us at:
www.footprinttravelguides.com.

Join us on facebook for the latest travel news, product releases, offers and amazing competitions:
www.facebook.com/footprintbooks.